Science Arts

2nd EDITION

EXPLORING SCIENCE THROUGH HANDS-ON ART PROJECTS

MaryAnn F. Kohl & Jean Potter

CHICAGO REVIEW PRESS

T0051304

Library of Congress Control Number: 2020934710

Cover and interior design: Jonathan Hahn
Cover photographs: Shutterstock
Interior illustrations: K. Whelan Dery

Printed in the United States of America
5 4 3 2 1

Dedication

In loving memory of my husband, Michael. —*MAK*

To Mary, with devotion and gratitude. —*JP*

Acknowledgments

Special thanks to Suzanne Marchisio, science teacher at Whatcom Middle School, Bellingham, WA, for her scientific interpretations of the art experiences as science editor for Science Arts. Thanks also to Suzanne's eighth grade 1992–1993 science students for helping write the scientific explanations found on each page of this book. The students of preschools and elementary schools in the Bellingham area also deserve to be recognized for testing our art experiments.

Special thanks from MaryAnn to:

Amy Cheney, student, Silver Beach Elementary School, for her development and submission of the art project, Crayon Creatures.

My late husband, Michael, and my daughters, Hannah and Megan, for their expert creative opinions and advice, and especially their love and support.

Special thanks from Jean to:

Thomas, my husband, for his constant encouragement and love. Archie, for the time I spent in writing, rather than walking him. Banff Springs Resort, where most of my ideas were written. Macintosh Powerbook, for making my life easier and more mobile.

Using the Icons

In the upper page corner of each project, symbolic graphics or icons are found which make the projects in *Science Arts* more usable and accessible. These symbols quickly help identify which projects are appropriate for specific needs and uses of each child and each parent, teacher, or care provider. The icons are sugges-tions. You should feel encouraged to experiment with individual techniques or to change projects to suit the needs and abilities of children, parents, or teachers. Discovery and experimentation are the key to learning and exploring science through art.

Age Suggestion

3+ Indicates a general age range where a child can create and explore without adult assistance. Children younger or older than the age suggested may also enjoy the project. This icon is an indicator of the difficulty of a project; younger ages suggest easier projects and older ages suggest more difficult projects.

Art Technique

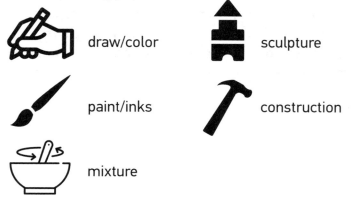

draw/color

sculpture

paint/inks

construction

mixture

Indicates the type of art medium or technique featured in the science/art experience.

Planning Preparation

easy   moderate   involved

Indicates the degree of planning or preparation involved in collecting materials and setting up this activity for the adult in charge, from easy to involved.

Outdoors

Indicates the use of outdoors in either preparation or in use. Some projects specifically require warm day, freezing night, area with sandbox, area with tree, etc.

Help

Indicates a child may need assistance from another child or an adult.

Caution

 Indicates the use of sharp, hot, or electrical materials where extra care and supervision should be observed with children. Adults should generally do the steps where the caution icon is positioned.

Science Concept

Just below the icons, a single science concept is provided to help the reader or the scientific artist understand the concept word inherent in the art experiment. For instance, when working with oil and water, the word *insoluble* is found near the icons because it best describes the scientific component of the art idea. Most of these science concepts are also found in the glossary (page 130).

Contents

3 • Motion and Energy   61

4 • Reactions and Change   87

5 • Nature and Earth   109

Introduction

Science Arts provides children with an exciting opportunity to learn basic science concepts through art experiences. Children ages 3 through 10 can explore the hands-on activities in each *Science Arts* experiment. While manipulating art materials, children are actually learning science concepts.

Children explore, manipulate, and discover art and science as an intertwined process rather than a final product. Thus, the product becomes an outcome of experimenting and experiencing, rather than the sole reason for the activity. The pure joy of discovery and taking an active part in learning is the main objective of *Science Arts*.

Science Arts appeals to the combination of the curiosity of science and the beauty of art. Each art activity has a science concept inherent in its process. Science experiments are often filled with interesting and amazing reactions, effects, and results. Thus, children are not only captured by the beauty and fun of the creation, but may also be fascinated and surprised with the science concepts.

Each page of *Science Arts* contains one experiment that includes simple instructions, clear illustrations, and suggestions for variations or extensions to enhance learning. Each is designed to be used by an individual child, by small groups of children, or independently or with some adult help. Materials needed for each experiment are commonly found in most homes or classrooms, making *Science Arts* ideal for home or school use.

"The fairest thing we can experience is the mysterious. It is the fundamental emotion which stands at the cradle of true art and true science."

—Albert Einstein

CHAPTER 1
Water and Air

Wet Paint Design

Diffusion

Diffusion occurs when paint molecules are crowded into one spot on the wet paper and the drop gradually spreads out in the water.

Materials

water
shallow pan
construction paper
cookie sheet with sides
tempera paint, thinned with water
eyedroppers
newspaper

Art Experiment

1. Wet the paper thoroughly by dipping it into the pan of water.
2. Place the wet paper immediately on the cookie sheet.
3. Drop different colors of thinned tempera paint on the wet paper using the eyedroppers.
4. Remove the painting from the cookie sheet to newspaper to dry.

Variations

- Instead of eyedroppers, dip other objects in the paint: cotton swabs, paint brushes, drinking straws, feathers, twigs
- Draw with colored chalk on wet paper.
- Use water-based colored marking pens on wet paper.
- Use watercolor paints instead of tempera paints on wet paper.

Wet and Dry Painting

Dissolve / Diffuse

As powdered tempera paint is shaken onto the wet paper, the paint particles are *absorbed* by the water and then begin to *dissolve*. The liquid paint will then *diffuse* and spread throughout the water, forming designs and patterns.

Materials

tempera paints, powdered
several salt shakers
water
shallow pan
construction paper
cookie pan with sides
newspaper

Art Experiment

1. Put the dry tempera paint into a salt shaker and shake it to see if the paint comes out. Do the same for the other shakers and paint colors.
2. Fill the shallow pan half full with water.
3. Wet the paper thoroughly by dipping it into the pan of water and place it immediately in the cookie pan.
4. Shake different colors of the dry tempera on the wet paper.
5. Remove the paper from the pan and let it dry on newspaper.

Variations

- Color a picture on construction paper first, and then apply water and dry paint from a shaker.
- Shake salt on the Wet and Dry Painting to see the crystals react with water.
- Sprinkle dry paint on dry paper. Then go outside into the rain and let the drops of rain spatter the paint.

Invisible Designs

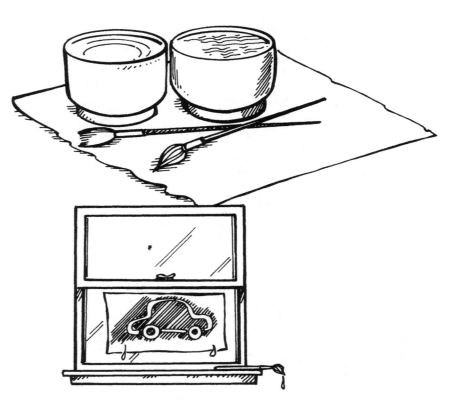

Insoluble

Oil and water are *insoluble*, which means they will not mix. When oil is brushed on the butcher paper, it is *absorbed* by the paper or soaks into the paper and will not mix with the water. Wherever there is no oil on the paper, the paper easily absorbs the water.

Materials

cooking oil in cup
butcher paper
brushes
water in cup
window or light source

Art Experiment

1. Paint with cooking oil on butcher paper.
2. Hold the design up to the light to make the art visible.
3. With a paint brush full of water, paint over the oil design. Paint on the untouched paper too.
4. Look at the way oil and water act together.

Variations

- Using a damp sponge, try to wipe the oil design away.
- Paint with watercolors on the oil and water designs.
- Draw with permanent felt pens on the oil and water designs.
- Draw with baby oil or vegetable oil on a cotton swab on copier paper.

Water Painting

3+

Evaporation

When water, a liquid, is brushed onto a surface such as a rock, it will usually change into water vapor, a gas, and enter the air. This process of change is called *evaporation*. When the air gets full of water vapor, it changes to a liquid again in the form of rain.

Materials

bucket
water
house painting brushes
outdoor area with sidewalks, rocks, or buildings

Art Experiment

1. Fill the bucket with water.
2. Dip the brush into the water.
3. Work outdoors, painting sidewalks, sides of buildings, rocks, concrete or asphalt play areas, swing sets, and more.
4. Paint designs or simply paint to cover objects with a bright, shiny coat of water.
5. When the water evaporates or dries, paint the objects again.

Variations

- Mark the water level in the bucket with a pen. Leave the bucket outside all day. Check the new water level after some of the water has evaporated.
- Wash doll clothes and hang to dry, observing evaporation.

Oil and Water Painting

Density / Insoluble

Oil and water will not mix so they are *insoluble*. When the oily paint is dripped on the watery paint, the two liquids stay separate and arrange themselves in layers according to their *density*. The watery paint is most dense and forms the bottom layer; the oily paint is less dense and floats on the water as the top layer.

Materials

2 colors of tempera paint
2 cups, approximately 500 ml each
water
cooking oil
paper
baking pan with sides
2 eyedroppers

Art Experiment

1. Mix one color of paint with water in a cup until thin and watery.
2. Mix the second color of paint with oil in the other cup.
3. Place a sheet of paper in the baking pan.
4. Use one eyedropper to drip spots of the watery paint onto the paper.
5. Use the second eyedropper to drip spots of oily paint on top of the watery paint spots.
6. Tip the pan back and forth to move the paints. The oil paint will float on the water paint to create unusual effects.

Variations

- Use more colors of paints.
- Use a larger tray or pan, larger paper, and a turkey baster instead of an eyedropper.

5+  Oil Painting

Insoluble

Oil and water won't mix because they are *insoluble*. The oily paint floats on top of the water in the pan because the water is denser than oil. Oil will not *dissolve* in water; oil stays oil and water stays water.

Materials

vegetable oil	water
tempera paint, powdered	spoons
cups	paper
shallow cake pan	newspaper

Art Experiment

1. Mix the tempera paint and oil in a cup until creamy.
2. Fill the cake pan about half full with water.
3. Spoon a few drops of the oil paint mixture on top of the water.
4. Use a spoon to gently swirl the paint.
5. Next, lay a piece of paper on top of the water and oil paint. Let the paper float for a minute or so.
6. Carefully lift the paper by one corner.
7. Immediately place the painting on newspaper to dry.

Variations

- Use Oil Painting designs as note cards, book covers, or wrapping paper.
- Create Oil Painting on waxed paper, paper plates, or plastic wrap.
- Add glitter on top of the wet oil paint.

Frost Plate

Crystals / Freezing

Water is a unique substance because it can be ice (a solid), water (a liquid), or water vapor (a gas), all within a close range of temperatures. When the petroleum jelly is placed in the freezer, water vapor in the freezer *freezes* and crystallizes on the jelly where it is easily seen in the drawing. The water vapor molecules slow down when cooled to 32°F (0°C) or below and arrange themselves in a regular pattern on the petroleum jelly as they form ice *crystals*.

Materials

petroleum jelly
clear glass pie plate
freezer

Art Experiment

1. Smear petroleum jelly on the glass pie plate.
2. Draw a design in the jelly on the plate with fingers.
3. Clean hands.
4. Put the plate in the freezer for 2 hours.
5. Remove the plate and look at the frost designs.

Variation

• Mix a little paint with the petroleum jelly and repeat experiment steps.

7+ 🖌️ ◔ 🌳

Frozen Paper

Freezing

When watercolor paint comes in contact with the *frozen* paper, it cools and nearly freezes too. This cooling slows down the movement of the paint molecules and the paint begins to freeze and behave more like a solid. If the paper begins to thaw or melt, the molecules of paint and water move faster and mix more easily, much like the usual behavior of paint and water.

Materials

freezer (or freezing day outdoors)
heavy paper
water

shallow pan
cookie sheet
watercolor paints and brush

Art Experiment

1. Dip the paper in a shallow pan of water until it's thoroughly wet.
2. Place the wet paper on a cookie sheet.
3. Place the cookie sheet and paper in the freezer or outside to freeze.
4. When frozen, remove the paper from the freezer and paint on the paper before it thaws.

Variations

- Freeze a variety of papers: paper towel, coffee filter, construction paper, copier paper.
- Draw with chalk on frozen paper.
- Paint with tempera paints on frozen paper.

Cube Painting

3+

Freezing / Melting

When the water and paint mixture is cooled to 32°F (0°C) or lower, it *freezes* or changes from a liquid to a solid. Then when the paint ice cube is removed from the freezer, it begins to *melt* because the temperature is higher than 32°F (0°C). The ice melts into liquid paint as it is spread over the paper with the craft stick handle.

Materials

2 measuring cups
plastic ice cube trays
water
2 colors of tempera paint

craft sticks
freezer
white drawing paper

Art Experiment

1. Mix one color tempera paint with water in a measuring cup and the second color tempera paint with water in the other measuring cup. Mix until thin and lightly colored.
2. Pour the paint into plastic ice cube trays.
3. Put a craft stick in each cube section.
4. Freeze the tempera water mixture.
5. When frozen, remove the cubes from the trays.
6. Hold the stick of the tempera paint ice cubes and paint a picture on the white drawing paper.

Variations

- Make the frozen paint cubes in a muffin tin or silicon molds.
- Make additional colors of ice cubes. Allow them to melt on a large sheet of paper. Observe the results.

Colored Ice Cubes

Freezing / Melting

When the colored water is placed in the freezer at 32°F (0°C) or lower, it begins to change from a liquid to a solid. In a short period of time, the molecules of water slow down until the water *freezes* in its solid state—ice. As soon as the ice is carried outside where the temperature is higher than 32°F (0°C), it begins to *melt* or change to its liquid state—water. Because the water is colored and not clear, patterns and swirls of colors mix and run together as the ice melts and spreads out on the paper.

Materials

variety of food colorings
water
paper cups
plastic ice cube tray or silicon
    molds

freezer
warm day
white drawing paper

Art Experiment

1. Mix each food coloring with water in a cup.
2. Pour the different colors of water in the individual compartments of plastic ice cube trays, filling them a quarter full.
3. Place in the freezer until frozen solid.
4. Remove the colored cubes from the trays.
5. Take the paper and the ice cubes outside.
6. Arrange the cubes on the paper and let them melt and mix colors.
7. Then dry the colored cube picture completely.

Variation

- Use 1 ice cube on each sheet of paper, and move the paper around so the cube does the painting.

Outdoor Spray Art

Diffusion

When water is sprayed on the painting, each drop of water thins the paint and causes the paint and water molecules to *diffuse* and spread out. The colored paint slowly spreads out in the liquid. The *diffusion* of the paint and water changes the results of using paint alone.

Materials

watercolor or copier paper
tempera or watercolor paints
paintbrushes

spray or misting bottle
water
clothespins, optional

Art Experiment

1. Paint a picture or design on the paper.
2. Carry the painting outdoors. Pin or arrange the painting on branches of a tree, a bush, or a fence.
3. Gently spray the painting with water. A misting bottle works especially well.
4. Observe the diffusion of colors as the water touches the paint.
5. Bring the painting indoors to dry.

Variations

- Place the painting outdoors in the rain and watch the raindrops diffuse the colors.
- Draw with water-based marking pens (not permanent) and spray the drawing with a light mist of water.
- Paint on wet paper that has been sprayed with water.

Chalk Float Design

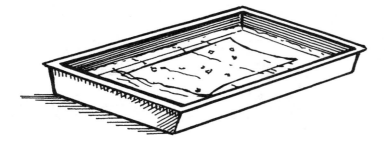

Surface Tension

A stick of chalk would normally sink in a pan of water, but chalk floats when it is shaved into tiny bits. Water forms a "skin" on its surface that holds up objects that usually sink. This "skin," caused by water molecules that line up and are strongly attracted to each other, is called *surface tension*. The chalk bits are so small and light that the surface tension of the water holds them up on the surface.

Materials

construction paper
colored chalk
kitchen grater
large cake pan half-filled with water
water

Art Experiment

1. Grate the colored chalk into very fine pieces on a piece of paper.
2. Sprinkle the colored chalk gratings on the water in the pan.
3. Carefully float the construction paper on the water.
4. Lift the paper out of the water and look at the chalk designs.
5. Place the chalk float picture in a place where it will dry overnight.

Variations

- Dip corners of a piece of paper through the floating chalk.
- Completely dip small pieces of paper into a bucket of water with chalk floating on the surface. Cover both sides of the paper.

Ice Structures

Freezing

When the air temperature is 32°F (0°C) or below, water will *freeze* into a solid form—ice. At these low temperatures, the water molecules move very slowly and gradually come together in a regular pattern called *ice*.

Materials

food coloring
water
large bowl
variety of molds:
yogurt cups, muffin pan, ice cube tray, candy molds
snow
freezing day outdoors

Art Experiment

1. Mix water with food coloring in a large bowl.
2. Pour the colored water into the molds.
3. Leave the molds outside to freeze.
4. When frozen, bring the molds inside.
5. Let the frozen molds thaw a little at room temperature to remove the ice shapes more easily.
6. Then take the ice shapes back outside and build a sculpture using the ice shapes. Use small amounts of snow as glue or mortar. Let freeze.

Variations

- Spray the sculpture with water mixed with dark paint in a spray bottle

8+ 🏠 🥧 Ice and Salt Sculpture

Melting Point

Every substance has a *melting point*, which is the temperature at which that substance will begin to change from a solid to a liquid. The melting point of ice is 32°F (0°C). But when salt is *dissolved* in water and sprayed on the ice chunk, the melting point of the ice is lowered and the ice melts more quickly.

Materials

large chunk of ice (freeze water in a large mixing bowl the day before)
baking pan
1½ cups (190 ml) salt
food coloring

1½ cups warm water (355 ml)
2 spray bottles, at least ¼ cup (60 ml) volume
scissors

Art Experiment

1. Place the ice chunk in a baking pan.
2. In a plastic spray bottle, mix 1/4 cup warm water with food coloring and 3/4 cup salt. Set aside.
3. Pour a cup of water over the ice chunk to make it slick.
4. Next, squirt the warm, salty, colored water on the ice chunk. Be sure the bottle is set on STREAM, not SPRAY. Squirt small amounts of liquid on different areas of the ice. (If too much gets on one area, rinse with clear water.) Try to form caverns, holes, cracks, and designs.
6. The ice sculpture is complete when the ice chunk is filled with designs and colors as desired.

Variations

- Make more than two colors of spray bottles for more color contrasts.
- Experiment with different sizes of ice chunks.
- Try this experiment without the salt and see what happens.

Color Bottles

Diffusion

Food coloring mixes with water in the plastic bottle in a slow process called *diffusion*. When the red food coloring is first dropped into the water, the molecules are crowded together. Then the food coloring molecules gradually spread throughout the water and the molecules have more space. The more the red color *diffuses*, the lighter the color of the water will be because the color spreads out more and more. Rolling the bottles and causing the water to move around speeds up the process of diffusion and the molecules move about more quickly.

Materials

plastic bottle with cap
water
food coloring

newspaper or towel for spills
table

Art Experiment

1. Fill the plastic bottle with water.
2. Add a few drops of red food coloring to the water in the bottle.
3. Place the cap on the bottle tightly.
4. Roll the bottle back and forth across the table and watch the color diffuse through the water.
5. Uncap the bottle and add a few drops of blue.
6. Repeat the rolling process and observe the new color.
7. Now add a few drops of yellow to the red and blue, rolling as before to see diffusion of color in the water.

Variations

- Mix blue and yellow only.
- Mix yellow and red only.
- Save bottles for decoration in a sunny window.
- Use other bottles, jars, and transparent containers.

Bottle Fountain

Pressure

The *pressure* of water increases with depth. The pressure is caused by the force of gravity, which pulls all things toward the center of the Earth. Small air molecules push down on top of the water causing a small water jet at the top of the bottle. More water molecules push down on the water lower in the bottle causing a larger water jet. The greatest pressure is at the bottom of the bottle, which causes the longest water jet of all.

Materials

empty dishwashing soap bottle   outdoor area
thumbtack or nail   towel
water bucket or sink

Art Experiment

1. Working outdoors, use the thumbtack or nail to poke holes in the dishwashing soap bottle. Start with three or four holes placed high and low.
2. Holding the bottle over a sink or bucket, fill the bottle with water.
3. Watch the water flow in different fountain jets.
4. After observing the water fountain jet design, add more holes until a desired fountain is acheived.
5. Add more water.
6. Watch the new fountain jet shapes.
7. Use the towel for any clean up.

Variation

- Stand a plastic bottle on a sidewalk outside and poke only one hole in the bottle. Then pour water into the spout and watch how far the water jets. Poke a second hole in a different spot and see how the second jet compares to the first. Continue adding holes in different places and comparing.

Bottle Optics

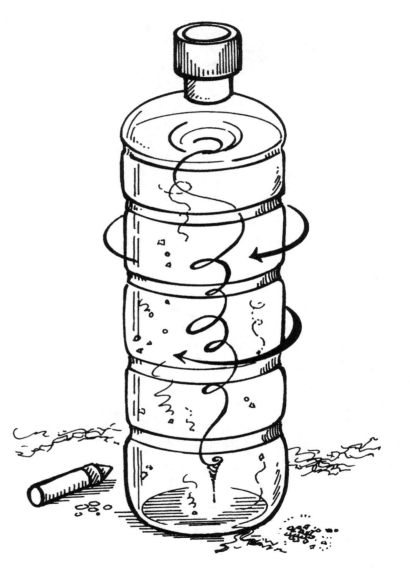

Density

Lightweight, tiny materials like crayon shavings and glitter that have the same *density* as water will be carried around with the moving water. These materials do not float on top of the water or sink to the bottom of the water but are suspended in the water and move around freely when the bottle is shaken and swirled.

Materials

large, clear plastic bottle
water
crayon shavings
glitter
metal or plastic confetti
bits of Easter grass

Art Experiment

1. Fill the bottle with water.
2. Add crayon shavings, glitter, or other small floating materials such as bits of Easter grass or plastic confetti.
3. Replace the lid and tighten.
4. Shake the bottle and watch the objects move.

Variations

- Color the water with food coloring.
- Use objects that float and sink and observe how they react to the moving water.
- Try to make a tornado movement by swirling in one direction.
- Experiment with designs and patterns in movement by tipping and shaking the bottle different ways.

Water Tube

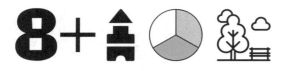

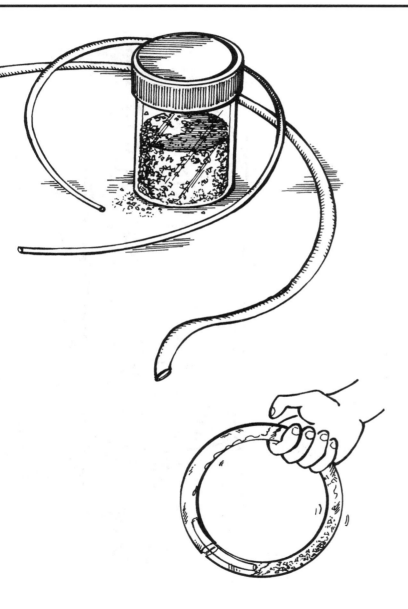

Density

The small bits of glitter are carried along in the water in the clear plastic tube because glitter has about the same *density* as the water. The glitter is cut into tiny pieces that are thin and flat. The water molecules push the flat surface of a piece of glitter, supporting it like a feather floating in the air.

Materials

3 feet (1 m) of 1-inch diameter tubing
6 inches (15 cm) of ½-inch diameter tubing
glitter
water
tape
outdoor play area

Art Experiment

1. Put some glitter in one end of the 3-foot length of tubing while holding up the other end.
2. Put enough water in the tube to fill it 3/4 full while continuing to hold the other end up.
3. Put the smaller tubing inside both ends of the larger tubing, forming a circle and a sort of plug. Tape in place.
4. Shake and move the water tube to see floating, sinking, swirling glitter.

Variations

- Find small objects like buttons, nuts and bolts, or marbles to fit inside the tube.
- Put soap and water inside the tube and shake.

Flowing Patterns

Symmetry

Liquids make designs as they flow, and create patterns as they flow into each other. *Symmetry* occurs in the water-and-cornstarch mixture when a straight line is drawn through the color drop and identical patterns form on either side of the line. In other words, the two sides of the design are *symmetrical* or matching halves.

Materials

shallow baking pan
water
3 tablespoons (40 ml) cornstarch

food coloring in squeeze bottles
stick or straw

Art Experiment

1. Fill the baking pan with water about 1-inch deep.
2. Add the cornstarch to the water one spoonful at a time and stir until the mixture looks milky.
3. Drop one drop of blue food coloring in the middle of the pan.
4. Next, slowly drag a stick through the color in a straight line. Watch patterns and designs form.
5. Now add one drop of yellow near the center of the pan, and one drop of red two inches away from the blue drop.
6. Watch new patterns and designs form while dragging the stick slowly between these two drops of food coloring.
7. Continue to create flowing patterns by dropping color in different places on the water and moving the stick through the colors.

7+ Paper Molds

Evaporation

Paper is made of tiny fibers tightly pressed together. Soaking torn paper pieces loosens the bonds between the fibers. When pulverized in a blender with water, the paper becomes saturated with water. This mixture is known as "slurry." Artists press the water out of the slurry and the evaporation process begins as the slurry dries. Evaporation is the process of water changing from a liquid to a gas. Warming the paper molds speeds up the process of evaporation by increasing the movement of water molecules. The faster the water molecules move, the faster they change into a gas, leave the paper, and enter the air. The paper molds are then dry.

Materials

Adult supervision required

measuring cups	spray vegetable oil
water	silicon candy molds
torn newspaper	sponge
torn colored tissue	paper towels
paper	
blender	
strainer	

Art Experiment

1. Mix 3½ (875 mL) to 4 cups (1 L) water with ¼ cup (62.5 ml) torn newspaper pieces in a blender.
2. Add some torn tissue paper for more color. Put on the lid and blend.
3. Strain the watery paper pulp, removing as much water as possible.
4. Spray some oil on the candy molds.
5. Press the paper pulp in the molds evenly.
6. Blot the pulp with a sponge to remove excess water.
7. Place a paper towel on top of the molds.
8. Place the molds in a warm place and allow them to dry thoroughly.
9. Remove the dried colorful paper pulp forms from the molds.

Variations

- Other items can be added to the blending stage of this project such as glitter, pieces of construction paper, or bits of flower petals or grass.
- The dried paper molds can be used as beads for a necklace, pendants, or holiday decorations.

Floating Sculpture

Buoyancy

Objects like corks and bits of wood float in water because the water molecules push up on the objects more than gravity pulls them down. The upthrust of the water is called *buoyancy*. *Flotation* occurs when the upthrust of water is in balance with the *density* of the objects. If an object is dense and pushes down more than the water pushes up, the object will sink.

Materials

floating objects such as:
    craft sticks, corks, Styrofoam bits, foil, sponges, straws, wood shavings,
    pieces of clay shaped like boats, thread, etc.
scissors
baking pan
water
towel to dry hands

Art Experiment

1. Fill the baking pan with water about 3/4 full.
2. Test the flotation of objects. Observe which ones float and which ones sink.
3. Begin floating objects in the pan. Add more objects until a floating sculpture is complete.

Variations:

- Stir the sculpture to watch objects move and change.
- Glue a variety of objects together with white glue. Dry. Float the sculpture in a pan, bowl, or tub depending on its size and the depth of water needed.
- Sponges can be cut into pieces and glued to form floating sponge sculptures.

Clay Floats

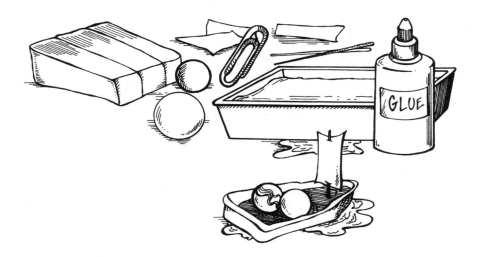

Floating / Sinking

Any substance like a ball of clay or a brick is *denser* than water and will *sink*. A ball of clay sinks because it pushes down on the water more than the water pushes up on the clay. To make the dense clay ball *float*, it can be shaped into a cup, bowl, or boat, which increases the volume of water the clay *displaces*. If there is a balance between the pushing of the clay and the upthrust of the water, the clay will float. Adding marbles or paper clips to the clay boat adds weight. If the water pushes up more than the weighted boat pushes down, the boat will float.

Materials

modeling clay or plasticine	paper clips
deep baking pan	toothpicks
water	paper scraps
marbles	glue

Art Experiment

1. Roll a small amount of modeling clay into a ball. Then press the ball into a flat piece. Next, turn up the sides to make a clay boat.
2. Float the clay boats on the water in the baking pan.
3. Experiment with placing marbles and paper clips into the clay boats to see how many items the boat can hold before sinking.
4. Make little sails of paper scraps glued to toothpicks to stick in the clay boats. Blow on the paper sails and see if the clay boats move.

Variations

- Find other materials that will float such as jar lids, Styrofoam trays, and bottle caps.
- Make boats out of reused aluminum foil.

Color Waves

Insoluble / Emulsion

The colored water and oil do not mix even though they are in the same container. They can be shaken and briefly combined, but they will separate again if left to rest. Oil and water are *insoluble* because they do not mix. When soap is shaken with the oil and colored water, the result is an *emulsion* or a suspension of tiny oil globules in the soapy colored water. The soap has simply broken the oil into smaller balls of oil, which are suspended throughout the water but are still separate from the water.

Materials

clear plastic bottle with cap
water
food coloring

baby oil
masking tape
dish soap

Art Experiment

1. Fill the bottle about ⅓ full with water.
2. Add some food coloring until desired color is reached.
3. Fill the remainder of the bottle with baby oil.
4. Put the cap on the bottle and tape securely.
5. Shake, roll, swirl, and experiment with the bottle of oil and water to make color waves and bubbles.
6. Remove tape, add dish soap, and retape cap securely.
7. Shake and see the difference the soap makes in how the suspension looks.

Variation

- Add other items to the Color Waves such as glitter, crayon shavings, or bits of plastic confetti.

Crystal Sparkle Dough

Crystals

Paint, flour, and salt will *dissolve* in water and can be made into a colorful dough. The particles of paint, flour, and salt break apart and spread evenly throughout the water. As the dough dries, the water *evaporates* and the flour, salt, and paint become solid again. Salt acts a bit differently than the paint and flour because after salt is dissolved in water, it forms *crystals* as it dries and becomes a solid.

Materials

equal parts of flour, salt, and water	3 cups
	3 tempera paint colors
bowl	3 squeeze bottles
spoon	paper

Art Experiment

1. Use a spoon to mix equal parts of flour, salt, and water in a bowl.
2. Divide the mixture into three cups. Add one color of tempera paint to the mixture in each cup.
3. Pour each cup of the mixture into a different squeeze bottle.
4. Squeeze the paint mixtures onto paper in any design.
5. Let the paint dry thoroughly to see the sparkles.

Variations

- Place the dough on wood, shells, or cardboard to create designs or objects.
- Spread the mixture with a spatula instead of squeezing.
- Vary the size of the holes in other squeeze bottles.

Straw Painting

 / 5+

Pressure

When the straw is dipped into the paint, some paint is pushed up into the straw by the *pressure* on the surface of the paint. Air molecules are pushing down on the paint in the straw, too. By putting a finger over the top of the straw, a balance of pressure above and below the paint in the straw is maintained. When the finger is removed from the straw, more air molecules push down on the paint than push up, and the paint comes out.

Materials

muffin tin
tempera paint, thinned and watery
drinking straws
paper

Art Experiment

1. Fill cups in the muffin tin ½ full with thinned, watery tempera paint.
2. Dip the bottom end of a drinking straw in the watery tempera paint, then hold a finger over the top end of the straw.
3. Move the straw to the paper and release the paint on the paper by removing the finger from the top end of the straw.
4. Follow the process several times until the Straw Painting is completed.
5. Let the paint dry.

Variations

- Enhance the painting by using a hair dryer to move the paints around.
- Add glitter, yarn, ribbon, or fabric scraps to the wet paint.

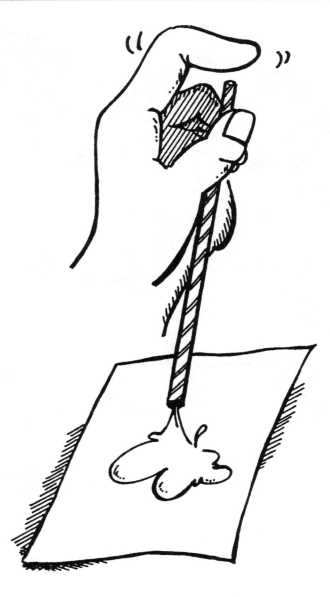

Streamer Rings

Wind

Lightweight materials like strips of newspaper or pieces of ribbon move easily in the *wind*. The direction of the wind is indicated by the way the streamers float. If the streamer floats out to the south, the wind is blowing from the north (called a northerly wind). Wind can be made by running with the streamers. Instead of the wind blowing air past the runner, the runner is moving past the air. The effect on the streamer rings is the same.

Materials

round plastic lid from coffee, margarine, or shortening tubs
scissors
strips of newspaper, crepe paper, ribbon, or cloth
tape (optional)
windy day outdoors

Art Experiment

1. Poke the point of a scissors into a plastic lid.
2. Cut a large circle in the lid of the plastic container. Save the rim or edge of the lid. Discard the center circle.
3. Tape or tie strips of paper, colorful ribbons, or cloth strips to the plastic rim.
4. Hold the decorated rim in the wind and watch the streamers blow.

Variations

- Tie many decorated rims to a swing set or tree branch and watch them blow.
- Tie metal objects to the bottom of the ribbons to make wind chimes when blowing.
- Tie several streamer sculptures to the center of a long rope. With a child holding each end of the rope, run side by side across a field or playground with the rope stretched between.

Wind Catcher

Wind

True windsocks are important indicators of wind direction used at airports and marinas. *Wind* is made up of moving air molecules, but the wind is invisible. *Wind* can be felt but not seen. The Wind Catcher makes it possible to tell which direction and how hard the wind is blowing.

Materials

round cardboard oats container
construction paper
crayons
glue
paper punch

crepe paper
scissors
string
windy day outdoors

Art Experiment

1. Cut the bottom off the cardboard cylinder.
2. Decorate the tube with construction paper and crayon.
3. Punch several holes ½ inch from the bottom edge of the tube.
4. Cut crepe paper about 3 feet (2.7 m) long.
5. Lace the crepe paper through the holes and tie securely.
6. Punch 4 holes an equal distance from each other around the top edge of the tube.
7. Tie a string through each hole, and tie the four strings together.
8. Tie the knot at the top to one longer string.
9. Hang the Wind Catcher outside. Watch the wind go to work.

Variations

- Tie strips of fabric, plastic, and other materials to the Wind Catcher.
- Create a Wind Catcher from a potato chip can, margarine tub, or other cylinders and containers.

Windy Wrap

Wind

Although air is invisible, it is made up of tiny particles called molecules. *Wind* is moving air molecules that push against anything in their path. The fabric and paper tied to the rope are in the wind's path and move when the moving air hits them. A lightweight material, especially if it has a large surface area, is easily moved by wind.

Materials

lightweight fabrics and papers	clothespins
permanent markers	windy day
clothesline, rope, or heavy string	

Art Experiment

1. Color the fabrics and papers with permanent markers in a variety of designs.
2. Wrap the clothesline through trees, around bushes, over benches, and on other outdoor environmental objects.
3. Clothespin the lightweight materials on the line so they will blow in the wind.
4. When Windy Wrap has been thoroughly enjoyed, be sure to clean up and recycle the materials.

Variations

- Test a variety of materials such as waxed paper, aluminum foil, and plastic bags to see which ones will blow most freely.
- Add reused items to the Windy Wrap such as plastic six-pack rings, bottle caps, Styrofoam trays, and paper cups.

Wind Chime

Wind

Wind is moving air molecules that push against the objects hanging from the stick which makes them swing and bump into each other. *Gravity* causes each metal object to hang down from the stick on a string. When the wind pushes the object one way, *gravity* pulls it back toward the Earth. The string keeps the object from falling to the ground, and the object then swings the other way, again pulled back down by gravity and hit again by the wind. The objects swing back and forth in the wind, creating sounds when the metal objects collide.

Materials

string
scissors
dowel or stick
variety of metal objects such as: nuts, bolts, washers, screws, nails, jar lids
outdoor area with tree

Art Experiment

1. Cut a pieces of string twice as long as the dowel or stick. Tie one end of the string at each end of the stick with enough slack to hang the wind chime from a tree branch.
2. Tie a piece of string to each metal object.
3. Next, tie each of the strings to the stick so the objects hang and bump into each other.
4. Carry the stick outside to a tree and hang on a branch.
5. When the wind blows, the metal objects will bump into one another and make noises or chimes.

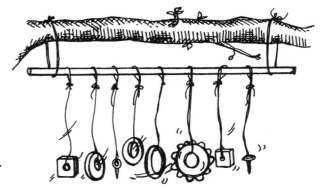

Variations

- Tie metal pipes with string to a stick or dowel. Hollow pipes make lovely chime sounds.
- Hang shells, pieces of driftwood, and other items from nature on a larger stick or branch.

CHAPTER 2

Light and Sight

Spinning Designs

Optical Illusion

When designs on the paper plate spin before our eyes, the brain perceives the spinning objects as a new and different image. The brain continues to see overlapping designs that appear to change shape and combine colors. The new perceived image is called an *optical illusion* because what we see is an *illusion* or impression of the actual designs.

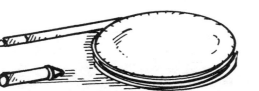

Materials

paper plates
marking pens
tape
Lazy Susan (plastic-and-rubber or wooden kitchen turntable)

Art Experiment

1. Draw a pattern or design on the paper plate with markers. Use bold lines and colors.
2. Loop a piece of tape on the back of the plate, sticky side out. Press the plate down on the Lazy Susan turntable.
3. Spin the turntable by hand.
4. Observe the changing patterns and colors as the drawing spins.

Variations

- Use tools such as a protractor, compass, or ruler to make designs.
- Draw on the paper plate with a marker with one hand while spinning the turntable with the other hand.

 **6+**

Hidden Coloring

Vision / Optics

The coordination of the hand and the eye are connected through the brain. Sighted people depend on their *vision* to control the movement of their hands. When vision is lost, it is difficult to make the hands do what they should, but it is fun to try.

Materials

scissors
shoe box
paper
crayons

Art Experiment

1. Use the scissors to cut a hole large enough to put a hand inside the shoe box.
2. Place a sheet of paper in the bottom of the box.
3. Draw on the paper inside the box without looking at the drawing.
4. Remove the drawing and see the results.

Variations:

- Write words, names, or messages inside the box without looking.
- Play a game where one person puts an object in the box, and the other person guesses what the object is just by feeling.
- Paint or draw while blindfolded.

Secret Pictures

Optics

When a picture is painted with lemon juice, it dries to an *invisible* design. Then, when the electric iron heats the lemon juice markings, the natural sugar in the juice burns and becomes a brown carbon substance. This browned juice is then seen as the secret painting or picture.

Materials

Adult supervision required
lemons
cup
paintbrush
white bond paper
iron
newspaper

Art Experiment

1. Squeeze the juice of one lemon in a cup. (Heating the lemon in a microwave for 15 seconds will result in more juice per lemon.)
2. Dip a paintbrush in the lemon juice and paint on the white bond paper.
3. Let the picture dry thoroughly.
4. An adult can place the drawing between newspaper and iron it until a brown design appears.

Variations

- Paint a Secret Picture for a friend or family member. Let them brown the picture with an iron for a surprise.
- Use Secret Pictures to write a secret message or give clues to a hidden treasure.

Stretch Picture

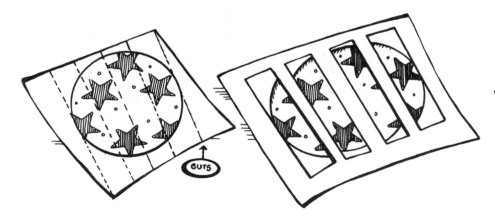

7

Optics

A Stretch Picture is an *optical illusion* or a trick the eyes play on the brain. The eyes are not accustomed to seeing a picture that is cut into curvy strips or strips cut and spaced apart. The brain receives this unusual image and tries to make sense out of it by "filling in the gaps" in the picture and trying to make it seem more like a normal picture. The brain may even think the Stretch Picture seems to be moving or wiggling when it is really holding still.

Materials

magazine picture   glue
scissors   paper

Art Experiment

1. Cut a magazine picture into four strips.
2. Arrange the picture on the paper leaving some space between each strip.
3. Glue the strips onto the paper. See how the picture has stretched and how it makes the eyes feel to look at the stretched picture.

Variations

- Cut a picture in more than four strips.
- Cut the picture in wavy or jagged strips.
- Cut a hand drawn picture instead of using a magazine picture.
- Use one piece of colored paper to cut out a shape instead of a magazine picture. Cut it into strips or pieces and "stretch" the shape. Glue the pieces on another piece of colored paper.

Dot Matrix Picture

Optics

The comics and funny papers are good examples of dot matrix pictures. The dots are so small that they can't be easily seen, but the brain combines the dots and sees new colors created by the mixing of only a few colors of dots. Creating a dot matrix picture is similar to a painting technique called *pointillism*, in which paint is applied to the paper in small dots or points only; no lines are used.

Materials

strong magnifying glass
cotton swabs
several colors of tempera paints in jar lids
white drawing paper
dot matrix pictures from magazine or comic book

Art Experiment

1. Look at the tiny dots in the dot matrix picture by using a strong magnifying glass.
2. Dip a cotton swab in a lid filled with tempera paint.
3. Then dab the swab on the paper, making many tiny dots and dabs. Use several colors, one swab per color. The dots will create a design or a picture when finished.

Variation

- Imitate the famous impressionist and pointillism artist Georges Seurat by painting entire scenes with dots or dabs of paint only.

8

Face Illusions

Optical Illusion

Human vision is *binocular*, which means that light enters through two eyes. When two images like the outline of the face and the facial features enter both eyes, only one image is seen. If the drawing is too close to the eyes, the two drawings seem to become one blurred drawing, image stacked on image. This *optical illusion* is like a trick played on the brain by the eyes.

Materials

paper
crayons

Art Experiment

1. Make a small dot in the center of the paper.
2. On one side of the dot, draw the outline of a face and color in a solid color.
3. On the other side of the dot, draw only the features of the face.
4. Hold the picture out at arm's length and look at the dot.
5. Next, bring the paper closer and closer to the eyes while continuing to stare at the dot. The two drawings should seem to join into one face.

Variation

- Create other combinations of two images on either side of the dot such as:
  ▸ moon with craters, shadows, rocks
  ▸ flower with bright tropical colors
  ▸ map with rivers, roads, features

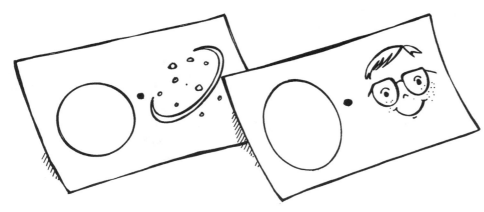

Tissue Color Mix

Pigments

The color in art tissue paper is made of chemical dyes called *pigments*. Each pigment absorbs some kinds of light and reflects other kinds of light. This is why things are seen in color. When different colors of tissue papers are mixed or layered with the liquid starch, they combine and create a new color.

Materials

colored art tissue paper: yellow, magenta, and bright blue
scissors
liquid starch or thinned white glue

paintbrush
white paper
water for rinsing

Art Experiment

1. Cut art tissue into a variety of shapes.
2. Dip a paintbrush into liquid starch and use it like glue to paint and stick tissue shapes to white paper.
3. Overlap shapes to create new colors. Rinse the brush in clear water often. This will keep the colors bright.
4. Layer the following colored tissues to make new colors:
   - magenta over yellow to create red
   - bright blue over yellow to create green
   - magenta over bright blue to create purple
   - combinations of all three to create black

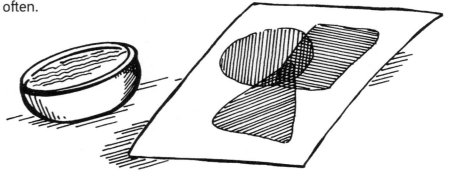

Variations

- Use starch to brush tissue pieces on clear plastic wrap. Then dry and tape the picture to a sunny window.
- Use liquid starch to glue tissue pieces to waxed paper.

White Light

When mixing the rainbow colors of light (red, orange, yellow, green, blue, indigo, and violet), the result is *white light*, just like from the sun. When the wheel spins, the eyes cannot keep up with the separate colored pie shapes, so the colors appear to blend. When the wheel spins it will look pale-gray unless perfectly pure colors were used in a perfectly correct balance. Pure *white light* is almost impossible to create, but the White Color Wheel comes very close.

Materials

white cardboard or paper plate
cereal bowl or coffee can lid
scissors
pencil

paints (red, orange, yellow, green,
   cobalt blue, indigo, violet)
paintbrush
protractor or ruler

Art Experiment

1. Draw a circle on the white cardboard by tracing a cereal bowl or coffee can lid.
2. Cut out the circle.
3. Draw seven sections on the circle using a protractor or ruler. Try to make them the same size. (This is the most fun of all!) Help may be needed.
4. Paint a different color on each section of the circle. Use red, green, yellow, orange, blue, indigo, and violet.
5. Poke a hole in the middle of the circle to fit on a pencil.
6. Spin the color circle on the pencil.
7. Keep it spinning and watch the colors disappear as white is created.

Variations

- Make a circle with only three colors and see what new color is made when the circle spins.
- Make a circle with any choice of colors and see what new color is made when the circle spins.

See It Cards

Reflection

The aluminum foil shapes are excellent *reflectors* because foil is smooth and shiny, almost like a mirror. Light that hits the foil will bounce back or *reflect*, sometimes bouncing onto another surface like a wall where the foil reflection can be seen.

Materials

aluminum foil
scissors
6-inch × 6-inch (15 cm × 15 cm) dark-colored paper
glue
sunny, outdoor area or bright light

Art Experiment

1. Cut the aluminum foil into different shapes and patterns, keeping the foil fairly smooth.
2. Glue the aluminum shapes shiny side up and close together on the dark paper.
3. Take the foil design outside or put it under a bright light to see the light reflect off the foil and onto other surfaces.

Variations

- Go outside at night and shine a flashlight on the foil cards, reflecting the designs onto a wall or door.
- Reflect the shapes into a mirror.

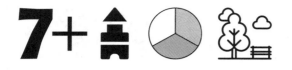

Shadow Time

Time

The Earth turns or *rotates* once each day, which makes day and night. Ancient people used a *sundial* to measure the turning or rotating of the Earth each hour and to keep track of *time*. By watching the shadow made by the sun with the stick during the day and marking its movement each hour, the turning of the Earth can be measured.

Materials

stick, twice as tall as flower pot
permanent marking pens or crayons
flower pot

sunny day outdoors
black marking pen or crayon

Art Experiment

1. Take the pot and stick outside on a sunny day and find a sunny spot. Turn the pot upside down and push a stick through the hole in the pot and into the ground.
2. At each hour, watch the shadow cast by the stick. Mark the shadow with a black permanent marker or crayon on the bottom of the pot.
3. If the sun shines all day, there will be twelve marked shadows on the bottom of the pot, one for each of the twelve hours.

Variation

- Tie a long string (about 3 feet or 1 meter) to a tall stick in the middle of the yard. Each hour, move the loose end of the string in line with the shadow made by the tall stick. Mark this shadow by placing a shorter stick in the ground at the loose end of the string (do not tie the string to the stick). After twelve hours, there will be a semicircle of sticks in the yard around the tall center stick. The next sunny day, watch where the shadow falls and tell the time by the hour.
- Draw designs on the flower pot with permanent marking pens or crayons.

Infinity Reflection

Reflections

A mirror is a smooth, shiny surface called a *reflector*, which means that light hitting the mirror will bounce off. When two mirrors are facing each other, the light from the person bounces off one mirror and onto the other mirror. The light will keep bouncing or *reflecting* from mirror to mirror, back and forth, creating many, many images of one person. Holding colorful cards up to the double mirrors will create endless reflections of designs.

Materials

2 mirrors
person to look in mirror
colorful shapes glued to cardboard cards

Art Experiment

1. Set up two facing mirrors so that they are almost parallel.
2. Stand between them and look into the mirrors.
3. Observe the infinite images.
4. Next, hold one of the colorful shape cardboards up to the mirrors.
5. Adjust and experiment with the shapes to achieve different infinite reflections.

Variations

- Hold other objects, paintings, and shapes up to the mirrors to experiment with infinite designs.
- Count the number of infinite images seen.

6+ 🖌 ◔ **Mirror Painting**

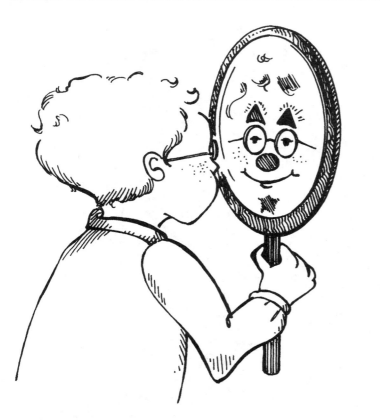

Reflection

When looking in a mirror, the light from that face bounces back to the eyes and a *reflection* is seen. A mirror is a perfect *reflector* because all light that hits a mirror bounces off. To be a good reflector, the material must be very smooth and shiny.

Materials

newspaper
hand mirror
tempera paints
paintbrushes

Art Experiment

1. Spread newspaper on the table.
2. Lay the hand mirror on the newspaper.
3. Look into the mirror.
4. Use tempera paints and brushes to paint a face and features on the mirror. Note: The mirror can be washed with warm soapy water, dried, and used again.

Variations

- Paint a hat, beard, jewelry, or unusual hair on the person in the mirror.
- Use a full-length mirror to paint the entire body.
- Paint any design on the mirror to enjoy the slippery surface.
- Draw with water-based marking pens on the mirror.

Cold Colors

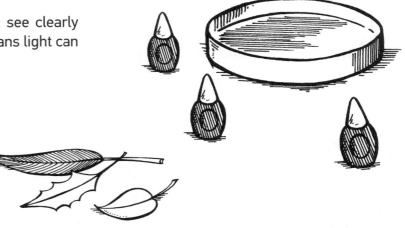

Transparent/Translucent

Clear water is *transparent*, which means light passes through it and we can see clearly through it. When clear colored water freezes, it becomes *translucent*, which means light can pass through the ice but seeing through the ice is not possible.

Materials

small, round, shallow jar
  lid with a rim
embroidery thread
food coloring
water

cup
collections of small
  natural objects: flowers,
  seeds, pine needles, bits
  of grass, weeds

freezer
scissors
cold day
tree

Art Experiment

1. Loop embroidery thread around the inner edge of each lid, letting it extend out and over the end of the lid to form a hanger. Do this for all the lids so they are ready to use.
2. Choose a color to mix with water. Mix the water and a very tiny amount of food coloring in a cup to make a light color.
3. Carefully pour the water into the lid.
4. Next, arrange the small natural objects in the water in the lid.
5. Carefully place the lid arrangement in the freezer and freeze overnight.
6. When completely frozen, take the Cold Colors outside on a cold day and hang on a branch.

Variations

- Work with only one color of natural objects and a matching color of water. For example, color the water green and find green natural objects to create the frozen arrangement.
- Fill the jar lid with bird seed. When frozen, hang in a tree for the birds to enjoy.

5+ 🖌 ⊘ Marker Color Filter

Filtering

In chemistry, filtering colors is called *chromatography*, a process that separates colors from one single color. The eye does not perceive that there is actually a mixture of colors in a marker that appears to be one color. *Filtering* the colors shows what colors make up the one color perceived in the marker.

Materials

white coffee filters
water-based markers (not-permanent)

table covered in newspaper
glasses, cups, or jars of water

Art Experiment

1. Choose one marker and one coffee filter to begin.
2. Spread the filter out on newspaper.
3. With one marker, draw a bold wide circle in the center of the coffee filter. Draw the circle like a small donut.
4. Next, fold the coffee filter into a cone shape. To do this, fold in half and then in half again.
5. Next, arrange the cone-shaped coffee filter on the jar of water with only the tip of the cone touching the water. Be careful the marker color does not touch the water.
6. Observe the water as it absorbs into the filter. What colors are filtered from the one color of the marker?
7. After the water is fully absorbed all the way to the outside edges of the coffee filter, unfold it and place it on newspaper to dry. The results will be even more evident when the coffee filter has dried.

Variations

- Repeat the process with as many colored markers and filters as you wish. You will need a cup of water for each coffee filter.
- When all filters are dry, use for other art projects.
- Create a butterfly with the filter using a pipe cleaner or clothespin to pinch the filter in the center.
- Create flowers from the filters and place in a dry vase or jar.

Light and Sight

Color Mixing

Paint colors mix together to create something for us to look at, and the eye perceives a new color that is different from the original colors alone. Color is what the eyes see by the way a color reflects or emits light. Colors don't really mix together at all! Color is a perception. The *color mixing* happens in our eyes and that message is sent to the brain.

Materials

plastic wrap, plastic sheet, or plastic paper protector
clear glue in a squeeze bottle or white glue
squeeze bottle food coloring or liquid watercolors and a brush
toothpicks

Art Experiment

1. Squeeze clear glue onto a plastic sheet forming a line that is a closed shape. Be sure there are no openings in the shape and that the line connect from start to finish.
2. Drop food coloring or liquid watercolors on the wet glue.
3. Spread the colors around with a toothpick. Filling the shape with glue gives more area for color mixing.
4. Set the design aside to dry completely, which will take three to five days.
5. When dry, gently and carefully peel a corner of the glue art from the plastic. Slowly remove the full shape.
6. Hold the glue art up to a window or a light to see the colors more clearly and brightly.

Variations

- Tie a ribbon or yarn to the glue art and hang in a window as a sun-catcher.
- Hang several glue art designs in a row on a long string and hang in a window.

CD Reflections

Reflection

The colors that can be seen on a blank CD are created by light *reflecting* from ridges etched into the CD. When light *reflects* off the CD, rainbow colors are split and reflected from the CD. Patterns can also be seen. A rainbow appears when the light is split into its seven different colors: red, orange, yellow, green, blue, indigo and violet.

Materials

CD
blank white paper or white wall
flashlight

Art Experiment

1. Place the CD on the floor, blank side up.
2. If there is not an open, white space on the wall, tape a piece of white paper to the wall.
3. Turn off the lighs in the room.
4. Aim the flashlight at the CD. Find the angle at which the the light from the flashlight reflects a rainbow on the paper or white wall.

Variations

- Go outdoors and use the CD to reflect sunlight onto a sheet of paper or a wall.
- In a dark room, look through a thin silk scarf or a feather at a bright light bulb. Observe the patterns and colors. Move the scarf or feather, and the patterns will move and change.
- Squint at a distant bright light at night. You'll see starburst patterns around the light.

Silhouettes

Opaque

Light travels in a straight path. The light from the slide projector cannot curve around the person on the chair or pass through the person. The person is *opaque* and blocks the light, casting a *shadow* on the wall. The shadow is basically the same shape as the person, but may be bigger or smaller depending on the angle of light hitting the person and the distance the person is from the wall. The shadow that occurs on the wall is called a *silhouette*.

Materials

bright lamp or flashlight	tape	white paper
blank wall	black paper	glue
chair	white crayon	
person	scissors	

Art Experiment

1. Place the lamp or flashlight on a table several feet away from a blank wall.
2. Turn on the light.
3. Place a chair next to the wall.
4. Have a person sit sideways on the chair so their profile can be seen.
5. Tape black paper on the wall so the profile falls on the paper.
6. Trace around the profile with a white crayon.
7. When complete, cut out the traced shape on the white line to create a cutout silhouette.
8. Spread glue on the crayon side of the black silhouette and stick to a sheet of white paper.

Variations

- Set objects on the chair such as a stuffed animal, statue, or a vase of flowers. Trace the silhouette of the object, cut out, and glue on white paper.
- Make Silhouettes with other colors of paper.

8+ Silhouette Show

Opaque

Light from the bare lamp travels in a straight line. When it hits the cutout paper characters, it cannot curve around them or pass through them because the paper is *opaque*. A *shadow* is created on the wall that is basically the same shape as the opaque paper cutout that blocks the light. Another name for the shadow on the wall is a *silhouette*.

Materials

lamp without shade
table
blank wall
chair or chairs

craft sticks or straws
paper tape
scissors

Art Experiment

1. Draw outlines of characters, people, animals, or scenery such as houses and trees on any paper. Cut outlines out with scissors. The cutouts are silhouttes.
2. Tape the silhouette cut-outs to a craft stick or drinking straw.
3. Set up the lamp near a wall. Turn on the lamp so the light shines on the blank wall.
4. Place several chairs by the light on the wall.
5. While sitting on chairs with backs to the light, hold up silhouette cutouts so their shadows show on the wall.
6. Perform a Silhouette Show on the wall. (Several people may be needed for holding the silhouettes.)

Variations

- Act out a favorite story, nursery rhyme, or tale.
- Make up stories to act out.
- Use real objects instead of cutouts for the silhouettes.

Flashlight Patterns

Opaque

Materials can be *opaque*, *translucent*, or *transparent*. *Transparent* materials are clear like the glass of the flashlight lens and allow all light to pass through them. *Translucent* materials, like the colored cellophane, allow some light to shine through them, but not all. *Opaque* materials, like the black construction paper, block all light and no light shines through them. When the flashlight's beam of light shines through the *translucent* cellophane, but not through the *opaque* black paper, colored designs are created on the ceiling.

Materials

flashlight	paper	scissors	masking tape
black construction	pencils	paper punch	colored cellophane

Art Experiment

1. Stand the flashlight on the black paper with the light side down.
2. Use the pencil to draw a circle about ½ inch (1¼ cm) larger than the lens of the flashlight.
3. Remove the flashlight and cut out the circle.
4. Next punch several holes in the circle to make a pattern.
5. Put the circle with the holes over the flashlight lens and tape around the edges.
6. Tape the cellophane over the circle.
7. In a dark room, shine the flashlight on the ceiling to see the colored pattern made by the cellophane and patterned holes.

Variations

- Cut other designs, letters, or shapes out of black paper circles and shine their patterns on the wall or ceiling.
- Cover the lens of a flashlight with plastic wrap held in place with a rubber band to see the unusual pattern made.
- Experiment with other colorful transparent materials.

8+ ⊤ ◕ ✋ Flashlight Reflections

Reflections

A mirror has a smooth, shiny backing and surface. The light that hits the mirror bounces off or *reflects*. Light bouncing off a mirror is called *reflection*, just like a ball bouncing off a wall. The light design bounces off the mirror and onto the white card.

Materials

small flat mirror
white cardboard
flashlight

other colors of paper
scissors
piece of tape

Art Experiment

1. Hold the mirror and the white card at a right angle to each other.
2. Turn out the lights so the room is darkened.
3. Shine the flashlight onto the mirror. (The light will reflect onto the card.)
4. Now cut a circle of paper to fit over the lens of the flashlight. Then cut a design in the middle of this circle.
5. Next, stick the circle design to the flashlight lens with a piece of tape.
6. Repeat steps 1 through 3, shining the light onto the mirror, which reflects onto the card, and observe the reflection of the design taped over the flashlight.

Variations

- Experiment with the results of different designs and also different colors of cards other than white.
- Cover the card with aluminum foil.
- Use a mirror in place of the white card so that one mirror reflects into a second mirror.

Color Viewing Box

Filter

Looking through colored pieces of cellophane changes the way the objects in the box look. The colored cellophane is a *filter*. When looking through red cellophane, a blue crayon in the box will no longer look blue. This is because the cellophane lets some of the light through but filters out the rest.

Materials

old file folders
scissors
shoe box and lid

colored cellophane or art tissue
tape

colorful small objects, such as small toys

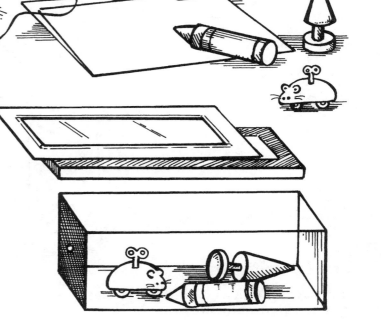

Art Experiment

1. Cut old file folders into cards about the same size as the shoe box lid. Make several cards this size.
2. Cut a large hole in the center of the lid and also in the cards, being sure to leave about 2 inches (5 cm) around all of the sides. It should resemble a picture frame.
3. Tape different colors of cellophane or art tissue to the card frames.
4. Cut a small hole in one end of the shoe box.
5. Put colorful objects inside the box.
6. Place the colored cards over the top of the shoe box and view the colors of the objects inside. It helps to have a strong light to shine through the colored cards and into the box.

Variations

- Walk around looking through a colored frame and see the world. See how colors change while walking.
- Cover old sunglasses (without lenses) with cellophane. Wear and observe the world through colored lenses.
- Construct a winter scene in the box and use a blue color frame.
- Construct a summer scene in the box and use a yellow color frame.

9+ 🔨 ◕ ✋ Real Camera

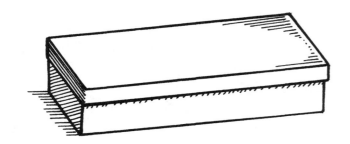

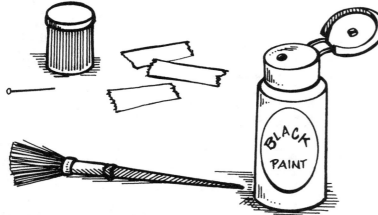

Photography

The hole in the box acts like the *lens* of a camera. The light from the window scene comes into the hole from many different angles traveling in straight lines. As the light from the window passes through the hole, it continues on until it hits the film. The film reacts to the light and reproduces a smaller version of the window scene on its surface. Too much light would expose the film and no image would be captured.

Materials

shoe box
black paint
paintbrush
pin
sheet of photographic film (not exposed to light)
completely darkened room with no light
masking tape

Art Experiment

1. Paint the inside of the box and lid black.
2. Make a pinhole in the center of one end of the box and put masking tape over the hole.
3. Switch the lights off and make sure the room is completely dark.
4. In the dark, tape a piece of the film on the inside wall of the box directly opposite the pinhole. The dull side of the film should face the pinhole.
5. Still working in the dark, put the lid on the box and tape around it. No light must get into the box.

6. The camera is now ready. Place the camera on the table with the pinhole facing the window. Place something in front of the window to take a picture of.
7. Being careful not to move the box, peel off the masking tape and leave the camera for 15 minutes.
8. Restick the tape carefully and, in the dark, remove the film and put it back in its envelope. Turn the light back on.
9. Take the film to a photo processing business to be developed.

Star Window

Constellations

Ancient and modern civilizations have always imagined objects, animals, and people in the patterns of stars in the sky that are called *constellations*. Each constellation usually has an imaginative story or tale that goes along with it telling how that star pattern came to be. One of the most common constellations is the Big Dipper.

Materials

clear night outdoors	pin
black construction paper	nail
newspapers	pencil
items to poke holes:	window
scissors	tape

Art Experiment

1. Look at stars on a clear night. Notice the different sizes of the dots of light in the sky and the patterns they seem to form.
2. Go inside. Place a piece black paper on a thick pad of newspaper.
3. Poke holes of different sizes through the black paper, copying the stars seen in the sky or creating patterns and stars from the imagination. Use the scissors, pin, nail, and pencil to make different sizes of holes.
4. When finished, tape the corners of the black paper to a window. The light shining through the window during the day will make the stars and patterns visible.

Variations

- Tape colored tissue or cellophane behind the holes to give the stars colors.
- Cut large holes or shapes and cover with colored tissue for a stained-glass effect or a light design.
- With a white pencil or chalk, connect the "dots" and form pictures, patterns, or shapes.

Window Scene

Opaque / Translucent

Materials that block light are called *opaque*. Materials that allow some light to pass through, like the tissues in Window Scene, are called *translucent*.

Materials

plastic wrap	colored tissue paper	paintbrush
tape	liquid starch (or thinned	
scissors	white glue)	

Art Experiment

1. Tear a piece of plastic wrap to fit a window. (For big windows, pull out a piece any size desired.)
2. Tape the corners of the plastic wrap to the table.
3. Cut bits of colored art tissue into shapes, characters, pictures, or a scene.
4. Use a paintbrush to paint the starch over the plastic wrap. Thinned white glue could be used as well.
5. Next, place colored tissue pieces into the starch on the plastic wrap.
6. Then paint over these colored tissue pieces with more starch. Keep adding tissue designs until finished.
7. Let the project dry completely, usually an hour or more.
8. Remove the tape or cut it at the corners of the plastic.
9. Tape the plastic wrap Window Scene to a window and watch the light shine through the translucent tissue.

Variations

- Make a Window Scene on waxed paper with starch.
- Make a Window Scene by sticking tissue paper to clear contact paper; then cover the scene with another piece of clear contact paper to seal the design.

Bubble Sculpture

Reflection

The colors on the soap bubble's surface are caused when light rays *reflecting* from the inner surface of the bubble interfere with light rays *reflecting* from the outer surface of the bubble. Some colors cancel out and disappear and other colors combine forming bands of color on the bubble's surface.

Materials

flexible, thin wire
1 (237 ml) cup strong dishwashing detergent (such as Dawn)

bucket with water, about 6 cups (1½ L)
3 tablespoons (45 ml) sugar

Art Experiment

1. Bend a piece of wire into any shape. Be sure to close the shape. (A circle or geometric shape works well.)
2. Bend the top of the wire to make a hanger or loop.
3. Add dishwashing soap to the bucket of water in about a 1:6 ratio.
4. Add the sugar to make the solution thicker.
5. Dip the wire shape into the bubble solution.
6. Pull the wire shape filled with bubble solution out slowly and look at the colors. Find the colored bands in the bubbles. Observe any change as the soap runs to the bottom of the shape.
7. Try blowing the solution into a bubble that floats away. Observe the shapes of the bubbles as they float.

Variations

- Use a wire hanger to bend into a shape. Dip the hanger into a large tub of bubble solution.
- Experiment with other objects to find which ones will make bubbles, such as canning jar rings, toys, slotted spoons, or a clean flyswatter.

CHAPTER 3
Motion and Energy

Shake Picture

Energy

For every action there is a reaction. Shaking the jar causes the paint to react to the action of shaking and to interact with the paper. It takes *energy* from muscles to make the paint move around in the jar. Whenever the paint hits paper it will stick in random patterns because the paper is *absorbent*, which means the solid paper is soaking up the liquid paint.

Materials

construction paper
scissors
liquid tempera paint
large jar with lid

Art Experiment

1. Cut the paper small enough to fit inside the jar.
2. Put the paper in the jar as shown.
3. Put several drops of paint in the jar.
4. Put on the lid and shake the jar.
5. Open the jar and remove the Shake Picture.
6. Let the painting dry.

Variations

- Repeat the above activity with two or more colors in one jar.
- Roll the paper into a tube and place in the jar covering the sides and shake.
- Before painting, put small pieces of tape on the paper. After the painting dries, remove the tape for a stencil effect.

5+ ✏ ◔ Paint Racing

Gravity

Toy cars, marbles, and balls all roll down the inclined easel board because of the force of *gravity*, but they are slowed down because of the force of *friction*. Friction will slow the rolling toy or ball as the surface of the toy rubs against the paint on the paper. Gravity also keeps the toys from rolling "up." Changing the thickness of the paint will increase or decrease the friction of the rolling object, making it faster or slower as it rolls across the paper. Experiment with gravity and friction by mixing different thicknesses of paint.

Materials

board from easel, with paint tray
  attached
long piece of butcher paper
newspaper

stack of blocks
marbles, toy cars, small balls, spools
liquid tempera paint

Art Experiment

1. Cover the easel board with butcher paper. Protect the floor with newspaper.
2. Make an incline with the board by propping one end up on blocks, with the paint tray at the bottom of the incline to catch rolling objects. (If there is no paint tray, use an old towel at the bottom to catch the toys.)
3. Dip one toy at a time, such as a marble or a toy car, in the paint in a jar lid or shallow cup.
4. Place the toy at the top of the inclined easel board and let it roll down making paint patterns.

Variations

- Raise or lower the incline to change the speed of rolling or change designs made by toys.
- Push a toy dipped in paint down the incline to force patterns.
- Using a spoon or squeeze bottle of paint, place blobs of paint on the paper on the incline. Roll toys, one at a time, through the paint blobs.

Streak Spin

8

Optics

The brain remembers the dots of chalk on the paper, but as the paper spins, the eye and the mind see rings on the paper because the eyes can't keep up with the spinning *image* of dots going around so quickly.

Materials

black construction paper
scissors
white chalk
pencil
masking tape

Art Experiment

1. Cut a 6-inch (15 cm) diameter circle from the black paper.
2. Use chalk to place dots on the black circle.
3. Poke the pencil point through the center of the circle. Use masking tape to secure the circle to the pencil on the underside.
4. Twirl the pencil back and forth between the palms of the hands and watch the white dots appear to become streaks.

Variation

- Draw many colors of dots on a white circle with crayons. Twirl between the hands.

Twirling Rainbow

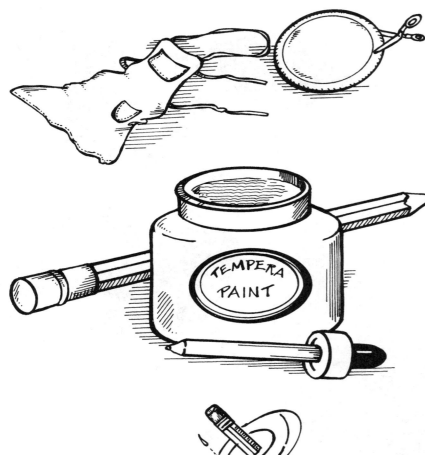

Centrifugal Force

When drops of paint are twirled on the plate, the paint spins out and away from the pencil, forming sunburst designs. The pencil is the axis and is the center of *centrifugal force*. The paint moves out from the axis in equal force from the center to the outside edge of the plate.

Materials

outdoor area
apron
small paper plate with edges trimmed away
pencil
masking tape
eyedropper
tempera paint, thinned

Art Experiment

1. Do this activity outside and cover clothing with an apron before beginning.
2. Push the point of the pencil through the center of the paper plate circle. Secure the paper plate to the pencil from the bottom with masking tape.
3. Place a drop of paint on top of the circle near the pencil.
4. Hold the pencil between the palms of the hands and twirl the pencil, spreading the paint swirling around the paper.

Variations

- Cut different shapes and types of paper to spin on the pencil.
- Use thicker tempera paint.
- Use food coloring.

Moving Pets

Optical Illusion

Two pictures moving very quickly in front of the of the eyes will appear to be one *image*. This phenomenon is called an *optical illusion*. There are really two pictures, but the brain sees them as one because they are moving so quickly the eyes can't keep up with the movement.

Materials

paper plate
scissors
crayons or colored pens
dowel, pencil, or straw
tape

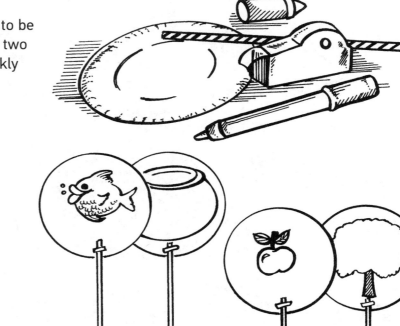

Art Experiment

1. Think of a pet and where it lives such as:
   - a fish in a bowl
   - a dog in a doghouse
   - a cat in a basket
   - a bird in a cage
2. Cut the rough edges of the paper plate off.
3. Draw a pet on one side of the paper plate circle.
4. Draw the house or bed of the pet on the other side of the paper plate circle.
5. Tape the dowel or pencil to the bottom edge of the plate, being careful not to cover the drawings with tape.
6. Hold the dowel or pencil between the palms of the hands and rub hands together to make the dowel twist quickly backward and forward. The pet will "appear" in its house or bed.

Variation

- Draw any two items which go together such as:
  - a hotdog in a bun
  - a smile on a face
  - an apple in a tree
  - money in a bank

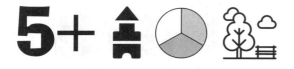

Spoke Weaving

Optics

The decorated wheel on the tricycle spins very rapidly. The human eye can't keep up with the speeding *images* so the brain blends the colors and shapes together into a blur of moving, mixing colors and shapes. As the spinning wheel slows down, the eye can begin to see separate decorations and individual colors.

Materials

tricycle or bicycle
paper
ribbon, crepe paper, yarn
outdoor play area

Art Experiment

1. Turn the tricycle on its side so the big wheel turns freely.
2. Create designs in the wheel weaving and tying the yarn, crepe paper, and ribbons in the spokes.
3. Spin the wheel to see the design. Be careful to keep fingers, loose hair, and clothes away from the spinning wheel.
4. Decorate the two small wheels too. Spin all three wheels.

Variations

- Decorate trikes and bikes and have a parade!
- Tie two colors of crepe paper, such as yellow and blue, in the spokes. Spin the wheel to see if the colors blend into a new color such as green.
- Decorate the spokes with an environmental theme such as twigs, leaves, flowers, and litter.

Marble Sculpture

⊘ ♦ **7+**

Gravity and friction

A marble is a smooth round object that rolls easily. Once the marble starts moving it will keep moving until something stops it. This demonstrates a law of physics called *inertia*, which states that an object in motion will remain in motion until another law causes it to stop. Two other laws that can get in the way of the rolling marble are those of *gravity* and *friction*. Gravity is the force that pulls all things toward the Earth and causes the marble to roll down the inclined ramps. Friction is the rubbing together of materials such as the marble against any surface, which slows the marble down.

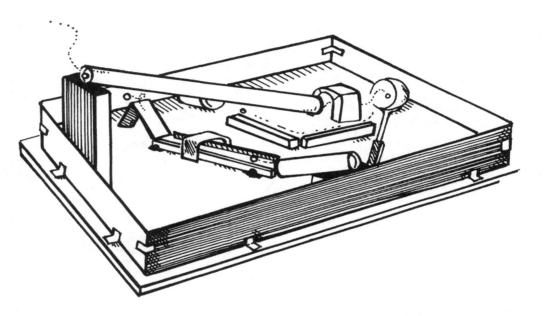

Materials

table	pipe insulation
marbles	plastic pipes
heavy paper strips	baskets
tape	yogurt cups
scissors	blocks
sculpture materials	cardboard tubes
playdough	cans

Art Experiment

1. Tape paper strips around the edge of the table to keep the marbles from rolling off.
2. Place other sculpture materials on the table and begin building a sculpture for marbles to roll through, into, and over.
3. Use inclines and connecting tracks and tunnels for marbles to follow. Playdough can be used to support tubes, pipes, and cans for tunnels and tracks.
4. Send marbles through the sculpture.

Variation

- In a box lid, draw a face. Instead of drawing eyeballs, punch or cut two holes where the eyeballs should be. Next, place two marbles in the lid. Tilt the lid back and forth, trying to put the marbles in the eye spaces.

4+ Color Spin Top

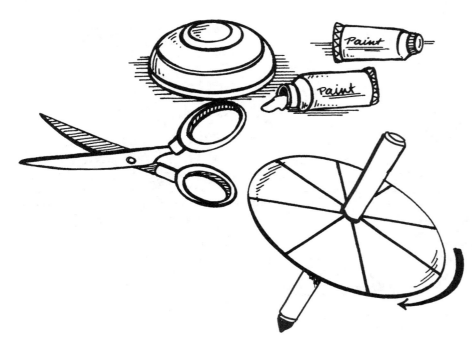

Energy/Gravity/Friction

Spinning a cardboard circle on the point of a marker is actually the same as a homemade toy called a top. When spinning a top, a force called *kinetic energy*, or *energy of motion*, occurs. As it spins, the top balances on the tiny tip, which reduces the amount of *friction* in contact with the table. Eventually, friction will begin to slow the top's spin. As it begins to wobble, the force of *gravity* exerts its pull and the top falls to one side.

Materials

jar lid or bowl, about 3 inches in diameter
colored marking pens
cardboard
scissors
newspaper
several sheets of white paper

Art Experiment

1. Trace around a jar lid or bowl on the cardboard to make a circle. Trace several circles. Then cut them out. Adult help may be needed cutting the stiff cardboard.
2. Next cut a small X in the center of each circle. Adult help will be needed.
3. Carefully push the tip of a colored marking pen through the X. Push the marker in about 1 inch. Repeat this process, making several tops, each with a different colored pen.
4. Practice spinning a top on newspaper to get the idea of how it works.
5. When ready, spin a top on white paper to see the designs the colored marker makes. Spin all the tops creating more designs in different colors.

Variations

To see optical blending of colors and designs on the spinning cardboard top:

• color boldly on the cardboard circle
• glue a circle of patterned wrapping paper over the cardboard circle
• draw pie-shaped lines on the circle and color in each section with a different color

Paint Pendulum

Gravity

A *pendulum* is a hanging object that swings freely because of the force of *gravity*. Gravity is the force that pulls things down to the center of the Earth. To swing a pendulum, an object is lifted up and then released. *Gravity* tries to pull the object down to the Earth, but the string prevents it from falling straight down. Instead, the weight swings back and forth, until the force of gravity overcomes the inertia created by the swinging. As the paint dribbles out of the cup, the pendulum paints a design caused by gravity and motion.

Materials

snow cone or watercooler paper cone (or
  standard paper cups)
scissors
string
dowel rod
two chairs
newspaper

construction paper
masking tape
tempera paints, thinned until
  runny

Art Experiment

1. Poke three holes in the top of the cup using the scissors point.
2. Lace string through the holes, gather the strings, and tie them in a knot above the cup.
3. Tie the cup with the string to the center of the dowel rod.
4. With the two chairs spaced apart and back to back, place the dowel rod on the seats of the chairs so the cup can swing freely.
5. Cover the floor under the cup with newspaper. Then place a sheet of construction paper on top of the newspaper.
6. Poke a tiny hole in the point of the cup so that paint can flow through it slowly. Then put masking tape over the hole.
7. Pour runny tempera paint into the cup until it is half full.
8. Pull the tape off and swing the cup slowly over the paper, releasing the paint and letting the cup swing freely.
9. Add more paint and continue making the pendulum painting until complete.

9+ ✍ ◔ ✋ Salt Pendulum

Gravity

A *pendulum* is a hanging object that swings freely because of the force of *gravity*. Gravity is the force that pulls things down to the center of the Earth. To swing a pendulum, an object is lifted up and then released. *Gravity* tries to pull the object down to the Earth, but the string prevents it from falling straight down. Instead, the weight swings back and forth. As the salt dribbles out of the cup, the pendulum draws a design caused by gravity and resulting swinging motion.

Materials

snow cone or watercooler paper cone (or standard paper cups)
scissors
string
dowel rod
two chairs
newspaper
black construction paper
salt

Art Experiment:

1. Poke three holes in the top of the cup using the scissors point.
2. Lace string through the holes, gather the strings, and tie them in a knot above the cup.
3. Tie the cup with the string to the center of the dowel rod.
4. With the two chairs spaced apart and back to back, place the dowel rod on the seats of the chairs so the cup can swing freely.
5. Cover the floor under the cup with newspaper. Then place a sheet of black construction paper on top of the newspaper.
6. Poke a hole in the point of the cup so that salt can flow through it slowly.
7. Cover the hole in the cup with one finger and fill the cup with salt.
8. Swing the pendulum and let go of the salt hole.
9. As the salt pours from the cup, it will mark a pattern of movement on the black paper.

Polished Crayon

Melting / Friction

When the crayon drawing is rubbed vigorously, heat is created from the *friction*. The wax molecules move faster and spread out or *melt*. When the friction stops, the crayon wax cools and the molecules slow down and hold the new, smoother shape caused by friction.

Materials

crayons
paper towels
paper

Art Experiment

1. Press hard with a crayon to draw a picture or design on the paper. Use lots of bright crayon, coloring hard.
2. Place the paper towel over a pointer finger and polish the crayon marks until they smear together, blend, and shine.

Variations

- Color with crayon on a sheet of paper. Then polish the marks. Next add chalk to the crayon drawing and smear both of these to blend chalk and crayon.
- Place paper on a warm surface, such as a buffet warming tray. Draw on warm paper with old crayons (paper peeled).

7+ 🔨 ⊙ ⚠ ✋ Crayon Creatures

developed by Amy Cheney of Bellingham, WA, age 10

Melting

Crayons will melt when heated. The molecules in the crayons move faster and spread apart, which allows the crayon materials to flow and fill the shape of the cookie cutter mold. Cooling returns the molecules to their solid state and the crayons continue to hold the new shape of the mold.

Materials

Adult supervision required

cookie cutters in a variety of animal shapes

heavy-duty aluminum foil

peeled, broken crayon stubs

cookie sheet

oven

Art Experiment

1. Cover the bottom of each cookie cutter with two layers of heavy-duty foil to prevent leaking of melted crayon.
2. Place the cookie cutters on a cookie sheet, foil-side down.
3. Fill each cookie cutter with peeled, broken crayon stubs. (Mix colors for a rainbow effect or fill with one color for a single-color result.)
4. Place the cookie sheet in a warm oven, about 200°F (93°C), for about 2 minutes or until crayon stubs melt a little and float but are not totally liquid.
5. Next, place the entire cookie sheet with cookie cutters into the freezer for about half an hour.
6. Remove crayon creatures from the freezer, and then from cookie cutters carefully.
7. Color with Crayon Creatures.
8. Clean cookie cutters with hot, soapy water.

Variations

- Use other shapes of cookie cutters such as circles, trees, or stars. Use for gifts, holiday decorations, or on paper.
- Use Crayon Creatures to create crayon rubbings.

Hot Sandpaper

Melting

Every material has a *melting point*, the temperature at which a material changes from solid to liquid. The melting point of crayon is very low and occurs easily in a warm oven. The melting crayon flows and spreads over the sandpaper and then hardens to a solid again when cooled.

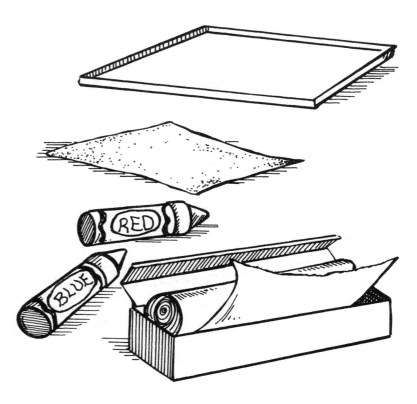

Materials

Adult supervision required
aluminum foil
cookie sheet
fine sandpaper (150 to 240 grit)
crayons
low oven, about 250°F (120°C)

Art Experiment

1. Line the cookie sheet with the foil.
2. Draw on the sandpaper pressing hard with the crayons.
3. Put the sandpaper drawing on the foil.
4. Bake the drawing for 10 to 15 seconds at 250°F (120°C) to slowly melt the crayon drawing. Remove from the oven and cool.

Variations

- While the sandpaper drawing is still warm and soft, press a piece of white copier paper over the design. Then peel off the paper for a sandpaper print.
- Drop bits of crayon shavings or crayon stubs on a foil-covered cookie sheet. Melt in a warm oven. Remove this from the oven. Press a piece of paper over the melted crayon and then peel off for a print.

6+  Baked Drawings

Melting

Every material has a *melting point*, the temperature at which the material will change from a solid to a liquid. The melting point of the wax in crayons is very low and occurs easily in a warm oven. The crayon wax flows over the paper when it is a liquid and then hardens to a solid again when it is cooled.

Materials

Adult supervision required
crayon
cardboard or heavy paper
aluminum foil
cookie sheet
warm oven

Art Experiment

1. Draw a design on the heavy paper or cardboard. Matte board scraps from frame shops work well.
2. Color and press hard with crayons so the colors are bright and applied in a heavy coat.
3. When finished, place the drawing on a foil covered cookie sheet.
4. Put the cookie sheet and drawing in the warm oven, about 200°F, with the door open and watch the drawing melt.
5. Carefully remove the picture when melted. Cool.

Variations

- Draw on a rock with crayon and melt the markings on the rock in a warm oven.
- Experiment with other papers and materials drawn on with crayon and warmed in the oven.

Motor Car Print

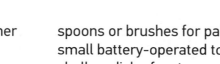 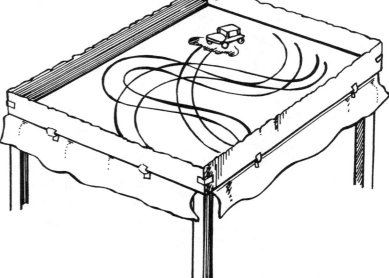

Electricity

A battery uses a chemical reaction to create *electricity*, a flow of charged particles that is one of the most versatile forms of *energy*. Because of the exchange of electricity through the toy car's motor, energy is transferred and used to move the car through the paint, creating a design.

Materials

table covered with large butcher
  paper or newsprint
poster board
masking tape
tempera paints

spoons or brushes for paint
small battery-operated toy car
shallow dish of water
paper towels

Art Experiment

1. Cover a table with newsprint or butcher paper.
2. Line the edges of the table with strips of poster board to form a fence that will keep the car on the table.
3. Spoon some paint anywhere on the paper.
4. Place a toy car on the paper and turn it on.
5. Let the car run through the paint making tracks as it goes.
6. Help the car go through paint and make designs.
7. To clean, turn the car off and have an adult remove the battery.
8. Gently rinse wheels and car in a shallow dish of water and dry with paper towels.
9. Replace battery and add more designs to this painting or begin a new one.

Variations

- Use an inexpensive remote-control car.
- Use any rolling toys and drive or maneuver them by hand through the paint to make designs. (Use only toys that will be used for painting as cleaning them is sometimes difficult.)

8+ ◆ Moon Scape

Gravity

When a ball or marble is dropped on the clay, the force of *gravity* is pulling the object downward toward the center of the Earth. Dropping an object in clay creates craters. *Craters* are giant holes formed when a meteorite smashes into a surface. Craters are round and have a rim around the edge made by material that is thrown out by the impact.

Materials

very soft modeling clay or plasticine	flat metal tray
round objects	tempera paints
ball bearings	paintbrushes
marbles	sheet of large drawing paper
tennis balls	
oranges	

Art Experiment:

1. Spread the soft modeling clay or plasticine over a flat metal tray.
2. Drop a ball-bearing or marble into the clay from different heights. Try 1 foot (30 cm), 2 feet (60 cm), and so on.
3. Try different weights of objects from different heights and see what types of designs can be made.
4. Work until a desired relief design is reached. The clay will begin to look a little like the surface of the moon.
5. Add other bits of clay for raised shapes to offset the holes made by dropping objects.
6. Paint the clay surface with a thin coat of tempera paint using one or many colors.
7. Gently lay a piece of large drawing paper over the painted clay.
8. Press and rub the paper's surface with the palm of the hand.
9. Peel off the paper to see the transferred moon scape print.

Note: Clay can be rinsed under the faucet until clean, patted dry with a towel, and used again.

Balloon Decoration

Static Electricity

Static electricity is caused by an electrical charge formed in certain materials. When a balloon is rubbed on clothing or hair, it becomes charged with electricity and attracts or pulls the little pieces of paper or granules of sugar towards its surface. The paper and sugar "jump up" off the tray and stick to the electrically charged balloon.

Materials

balloons, blown up and tied
lightweight items:
- paper confetti
- glitter
- sequins
- sugar, salt

tray or baking pan

Art Experiment

1. Sprinkle lightweight items into the tray, such as bits of torn paper, confetti, sugar, and sequins.
2. Rub a balloon against clothes or hair. (Hint: wool works very well.)
3. Hold the balloon just above the decorations in the tray. This is the best part!
4. Observe how the pieces jump and cling to the statically charged balloon.
5. For a more heavily decorated balloon, roll the balloon directly in decorations or sprinkle them on the balloon.
6. Continue decorating balloons in this way until satisfied.

Variations

- Make the balloons fit a special holiday or theme, such as:
  ‣ silver and black balloons with gold and silver bits for an outer space theme
  ‣ red and green balloons with gold sequins and ribbon bits for winter holidays
  ‣ pastel balloons with chopped Easter grass and dyed eggshell bits for spring
  ‣ light blue and white balloons with sugar crystals and silver sequins for ice and snow

6+  Dancing Rabbits

Static Electricity

Static electricity is created when particles in the plastic cutting board become charged by rubbing the board with silk or flannel. The board becomes positively charged and the paper bits become negatively charged. Since opposites attract, the negative paper bits are pulled toward the positive board because the paper is attracted to the charge in the board. The paper bits "jump up" and stick to the board.

Materials

2 thick books	scissors
plastic or acrylic cutting board	scrap of flannel or silk
paper	table

Art Experiment

1. Place two thick books several inches apart on a table.
2. Rest a plastic cutting board from one book to the other.
3. Draw, color, and cut out several small pieces of paper in rabbit shapes (or any other shapes).
4. Place them under the cutting board.
5. Rub the top of the board with the fabric scrap.
6. Watch the paper rabbits dance!

Variation

- Add other materials under the board, such as chopped Easter grass, confetti, glitter, and pieces of art tissue.

Magnet Painting

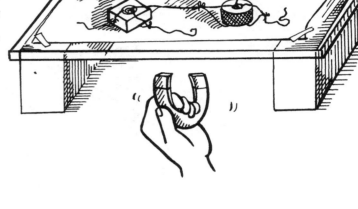

Magnetism

Magnetism is a property of some metals such as iron. Many objects around the house such as washers, nuts, bolts, and screws are partly made of iron and will be attracted to a magnet. The force from the magnet can be felt right through many materials, such as acrylic. When the magnet is moved under the acrylic sheet, objects with iron in them will be moved around above the sheet.

Materials

blocks	washers
11-inch × 14-inch (28 cm × 36 cm)	nuts
piece of acrylic	bolts
paper	embroidery floss or thread
tape	tempera paint
metal objects	strong magnet

Art Experiment

1. Place an acrylic sheet across two large blocks with enough room under the sheet to move hands.
2. Tape the paper on top of the acrylic sheet.
3. Tie varying lengths of embroidery floss to washers and nuts.
4. Dip the washers or other metal objects in paint and lay them on the paper.
5. Hold a magnet against the underside of the acrylic sheet and begin moving the magnet.
6. The magnet will "paint" with the metal objects and embroidery floss as they move over the paper.
7. Remove the objects, dip again in more paint, and continue painting until design is complete.

Variations

- Spoon blobs of paint on the paper and drag the objects through the paint with the magnet.
- Insert a marker through a nut. Place the nut and marker on top of the washer so that marker tip is exposed. Tape the marker, nut, and washer together. Move the magnet underneath the acrylic sheet to explore drawing with the marker in the nut.

Magnetism

Magnetism is a force that causes certain materials to be drawn together or pushed apart. Common objects that contain iron, like paper clips, are attracted to a magnet. By attaching cut-out shapes to a paper clip, the shapes can be moved around with a magnet through the box lid because the magnetic force is strong enough to work through thin cardboard.

Materials

colored markers	tape
box lid	paper clips
drawing paper	magnet
scissors	

Art Experiment

1. Draw and color an oval in the box lid to represent a face shape.
2. On the paper, draw and color facial features including eyes, hair, mouth, and nose. Cut these out.
3. Tape paper clips on the backs of each of the facial features.
4. Put all the facial features in the box, paper clip side down.
5. Hold a magnet under the box lid and move the features into place to make a complete face.

Variations

- Add additional features such as ears, hat, mustache, crown, ribbons, glasses, and others.
- Create other characters in box lids such as a clown, monster, astronaut, or performer.
- Draw other ideas with features to match such as a bowl with fruit, a bank with money, or a garden with flowers.

Metallic Design

⚠ ✋ ◔ ⚒ 8+

Magnetism

Magnetism is a property of some metals such as the iron in steel wool. The pattern formed by the bits of iron cut from steel wool shows the lines of force around the magnet. A piece of paper will not block the magnetic force and the filings line up along the lines of force making patterns.

Materials

Adult supervision required

fine steel wool
old scissors
magnet

heavy paper or light cardboard
clear, plastic fixative spray

Art Experiment:

1. An adult should cut the steel wool into tiny pieces with the old scissors.
2. Place the magnet on the table. Place a sheet of heavy paper over the magnet.
3. Sprinkle lots of steel wool pieces on the paper and watch them move into a pattern.
4. Move the paper over the magnet until a desired pattern is achieved. Or, move the magnet around to achieve different patterns.

Variations

- Use two bar magnets to make patterns as the poles attract or repel each other.
- Add other metal objects under the paper with the magnets. These pieces may become magnetized and make the patterns more dramatic.

9

Magnetic Stage Play

Magnetism

Magnetism is a force that causes certain materials to be drawn together or pushed apart. The force of magnetism can even travel through thin cardboard. Common objects that contain iron, such as paper clips, are attracted to a magnet. By attaching cut-out figures to a paper clip, the attraction of the magnet to the paper clip moves the figures around through the cardboard shoe box.

Materials

construction paper
colored markers
scissors
paper clips

glue or tape
shoe box
magnets

Art Experiment

1. On the construction paper, draw and cut out several characters for a play.
2. Tape or glue tabs made from construction paper on the base of each character.
3. Tape or glue paper clips to the bottom of each tab. The characters are now ready for the play.
4. Turn the shoe box on its side for a stage.
5. Place the characters on the top side of the box.
6. Use a magnet inside the box to move the characters back and forth on the box stage. The magnet will attract or hold to the paper clip through the shoe box and move the characters without touching them.
7. Make up a story and have the paper characters act it out.

Magnetic Designs

Magnetism

Magnetism is a property of some metals such as the iron filings. The pattern formed by the iron filings shows the lines of force from the magnet. A magnet has ends, called poles. One end, the north pole, is *attracted* to the other end, the south pole. The lines of magnetic force can be seen between the poles of the magnet when iron filings are sprinkled on white paper with the magnet underneath. When like poles of bar magnets are placed together they *repel*, or push away from each other. Attracting and repelling magnets show patterns with the iron filings.

Materials

Adult supervision required

bar magnets
large white paper

iron filings
other magnets (optional)

Art Experiment

1. Lay a bar magnet under a heavy sheet of white paper.
2. Sprinkle iron filings over the paper.
3. Watch patterns form in the filings as the magnet is moved under the paper.
4. Move the magnet to different spots under the paper to explore how many patterns can be formed.

Variations

- Lay two magnets with like poles almost together (that is, with the two *N*s or the two *S*s almost together).
- Place the bar magnets with opposite poles together (that is, with the *N* from one almost touching the *S* from the other).

CHAPTER 4
Reactions and Change

Candle Coloring

Adhesion / Cohesion

The watercolors will *adhere* or soak into the paper, but not where it is covered with candle wax. The watercolors are attracted to the paper by a force called *adhesion*. But the watercolors stay separate from the candle-wax drawing by a stronger force called *cohesion*. (See page 90, White Resist.)

Materials

newspaper
old candles
white drawing paper
watercolors
paintbrush

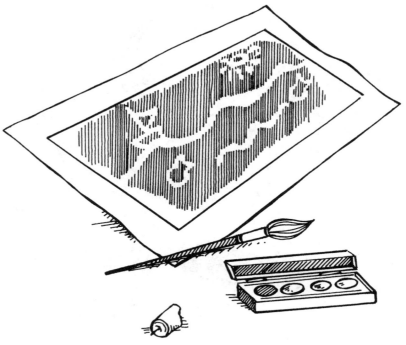

Art Experiment

1. Cover the table with newspaper.
2. Draw with the candle on white paper, pressing firmly.
3. Next, paint over the candle markings with watercolor paints.

Variations

- Draw with crayon and paint over this with black or dark purple tempera paint thinned with water.
- Use bright colors and press hard with crayon until the sheet of paper is entirely covered with crayon. Then paint over this with thick black paint. Dry. Scratch a design through the black paint with scissors or a paper clip.

White Resist

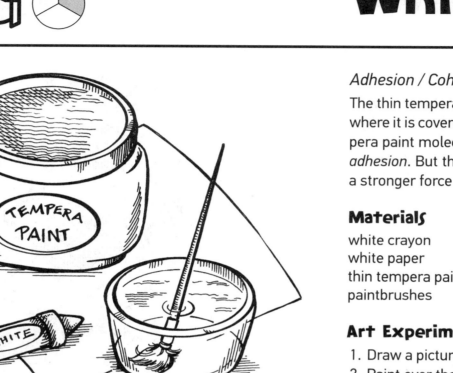

Adhesion / Cohesion

The thin tempera paint will *adhere* or soak into the paper, but not where it is covered with wax from the white crayon. The thin tempera paint molecules are attracted to the paper by a force called *adhesion*. But the paint stays separate from the waxed paper by a stronger force called *cohesion*. (See page 89, Candle Coloring.)

Materials

white crayon
white paper
thin tempera paint in cups
paintbrushes

Art Experiment

1. Draw a picture with white crayon on white paper.
2. Paint over the drawing with thinned tempera paint. Dry.

Variations

- Draw with many colors of crayons for a crayon resist.
- Experiment with black paint as compared to yellow paint.

Immiscibles

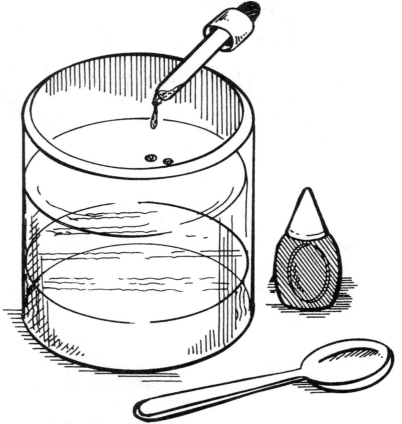

Immiscible

Oil and water are *immiscible* which means they will not mix. Oil and water stay separate even when shaken, stirred, or blended. The food coloring consists of mostly water and therefore will not mix with the oil. As soon as the food coloring is pushed through the oil and touches the water, it *diffuses* throughout the water in a burst of color. Food coloring and water are *miscible*, which means they can mix.

Materials

water   clear glass jar
cooking oil   eyedropper
food coloring   spoon

Art Experiment

1. Pour a little water into the jar.
2. Pour cooking oil on top of the water and watch them separate into layers.
3. Try stirring them together. Then let stand and separate again.
4. Using the eyedropper, carefully drop one or two drops of food color into the oil. The color will sit in tiny balls because food color is immiscible with oil.
5. Push the color balls into the water with a spoon.
6. Watch them burst into a cloud of color.

Variations

- Experiment with kitchen utensils to break up the color balls, such as an eggbeater, wire whisk, or fork.
- Use a watercolor paintbrush dipped into the color balls and see if it is possible to paint with them on paper.

9+ 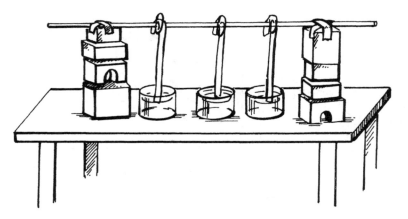 Chromatography

Chromatography

The process of separating colors or *pigments* is called *chromatography*. The paper strips absorb colored water from the jars and the colors are carried up the absorbent paper strip, dissolving as they absorb. The different colored pigments in each jar travel at different speeds and will separate into different bands of color. The pigments that dissolve quickly move up the paper the farthest and fastest. Pigments that dissolve slowly travel only a short distance and take the longest. Some of the inks and food coloring contain many pigments and will have many bands of color separating on the paper strip. Other inks and food coloring contain only one pigment and will have only one band of separated color on the paper strip.

Materials

dowel rod	jars
2 stacks of blocks	paper clips
masking tape	absorbent paper
inks or food coloring	eyedropper

Art Experiment

1. Suspend the dowel between two stacks of blocks over a table. Tape to hold.
2. Mix two or more of the inks or food colors into separate jars.
3. Use paper clips to clip strips of absorbent paper to the dowel, one strip for each jar.
4. Drop a small drop of color on the end of each strip.
5. Hang strips with ends just touching the water in the jars. Colors will travel up the strip and separate into colored bands.

Variations

- Drop a dot of color in the middle of a coffee filter and watch the colors separate. Dry.
- Moisten a paper towel. Drop a dot of color on the wet towel and watch the colors separate. Dry.

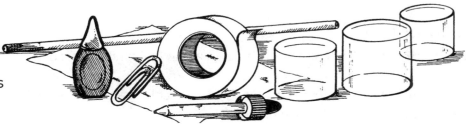

Erupting Colors

Solubility / Emulsion

Milk contains water and fat. These two substances do not mix because they are *insoluble*. Even though the milk looks like one substance, it is really separate water and fat. Detergent is a substance that will mix with water or fat, creating an *emulsion*. When detergent is dropped into milk, one end of the detergent molecule attaches to fat in the milk and the other end of the detergent molecule attaches to the water, which causes a churning effect.

Materials

cake pan with edges
milk
food coloring
liquid dishwashing detergent

Art Experiment

1. Pour milk into the cake pan until the bottom is covered.
2. Sprinkle several drops of food coloring on the milk.
3. Add a few drops of dishwashing detergent in the centers of the largest drops of coloring.
4. Watch the resulting eruption of colors.
5. If erupting slows down, try adding more food coloring and then more detergent. If the experiment will not work after a while, begin again with clean milk and new drops of color and detergent.
6. When experiment is complete, the pan washes easily in warm water.

Variations

- Make smaller experiments in custard cups and try different combinations of colors to see what new colors can be created.
- Use a clear baking pan. Have someone hold the experiment above eye level and watch the erupting colors from the bottom of the pan.

9+ The Volcano

Pressure / Gases

Baking soda reacts with vinegar to produce *carbon dioxide gas* which builds up enough *pressure* to force the foaming liquid out of the top of the bottle.

Materials

soda bottle
baking pan
moist soil
1 tablespoon (15 ml) baking soda
1 cup (250 ml) vinegar
red food coloring

Art Experiment

1. Place the baking pan on the grass and set the soda bottle in the center of the pan.
2. Mound and shape the moist soil around the bottle to form a mountain. Bring the soil right up to the top of the bottle's opening but do not get soil inside the bottle.
3. Pour 1 tablespoon (15 ml) baking soda into the bottle.
4. Color 1 cup (250 ml) vinegar with the red food coloring.
5. Pour the colored vinegar into the bottle. Stand back and watch red foam spray out the top and down the mountain of dirt like lava from a volcano.

Variation

• Explore adding additional colors to the mixture.

Crystal Design

⚠ 🖐 ◔ ⚗ **9+**

Crystals

Before salt is ground into the grains commonly used in food, salt is a large chunk and is a *crystal*. However, salt is usually seen when it is ground into smaller *crystals*. When the salt crystals are dissolved in the hot water, the molecules of salt spread throughout the water. Then, as the water *evaporates*, the salt molecules line up in a regular pattern to form a crystal again. Sometimes, if the conditions are just right, a really big, block-shaped crystal will form.

Materials

Adult supervision required

pipe cleaner
clear cup
½ cup (125 ml) hot water
⅓ cup (80 ml) salt

spoon
pencil
string

Art Experiment

1. Bend a pipe cleaner in any shape.
2. Pour ½ cup (125 ml) of very hot water into the clear cup.
3. Add about ⅓ cup (80 ml) salt to the water a spoonful at a time. Stir and dissolve after each spoonful. Add salt until no more will dissolve.
4. Curl the unbent end of the pipe cleaner around the middle of a pencil.
5. Place the pencil across the top of the cup. Be sure the pipe cleaner hangs deep into the hot, salty water.
6. Move this hot, crystal-growing cup into a place where it will not be disturbed and where it can be watched closely.
7. After a few hours, signs of crusty crystals will appear on the pipe cleaner.
8. Watch the crystals change each day. When most of the liquid is gone from the cup, remove the pipe cleaner from the cup and slide it off the pencil.
9. Carefully tie a string onto the top of the crystal shape and hang it where it can be seen and enjoyed.

Variation

- Add food coloring to the water in step 2.

4+ Crystal Paint

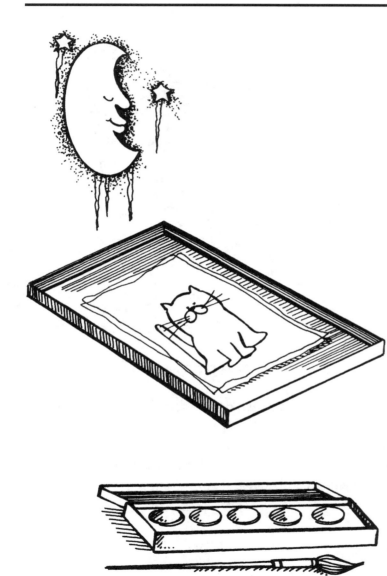

Crystals / Freezing

First the watercolor paints *diffuse* into the clear water on the paper, which causes the colors to run together. When the paper is placed in the freezer, the molecules of colored water slow down until they change from liquid to solid. This begins to occur at the *freezing* point of water, which is 32°F (0°C). When the molecules of colored water line up in a regular pattern, the colored water forms ice *crystals*.

Materials

water
watercolor paint and brushes
white drawing paper
plastic wrap
cookie sheet
freezing night or freezer

Art Experiment

1. Paint clear water all over the white drawing paper.
2. Then paint the wet paper with watercolor paint, letting colors run together.
3. Immediately cover the wet painting with a sheet of plastic wrap. Place on a cookie sheet.
4. Leave the painting outside in freezing weather, or place in the freezer.
5. Next day, pull the plastic wrap off the frozen painting and observe the crystal creation.

Crystal Bubbles

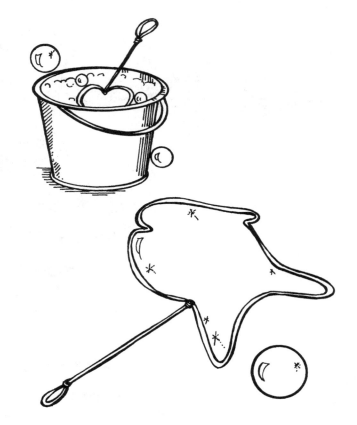

4+

Freezing / Crystals

At normal room temperature bubble soap is a *liquid*, but if you cool it enough or freeze it, it will become a *solid*. In the right conditions *crystals* will form when a bubble freezes and the molecules in the bubble arrange themselves in a pattern. If the bubble is cooled slowly, the molecules have time to line up just right and form *crystals*.

Materials

3–4 tablespoons (45–60 ml) of soap flakes or soap powder (Fels or Ivory)
4 cups (1 L) hot water
1 tablespoon sugar.
firm but bendable wire

Art Experiment

1. Make extra-strong bubble solution by combining the soap flakes or powder with hot water. Let stand for several days. Then add 1 tablespoon of sugar and stir.
2. Bend the wire into any shape. Be sure to "close" the shape.
3. Go outside on a very cold day, 32°F (0°C) or colder, when there is no wind.
4. Dip a bubble blower into the soap mixture and gently blow a large bubble. Try to not let the bubble blow away.
5. The bubble should begin to freeze, with tiny crystals forming over the surface.
6. The bubble will freeze completely into an ice crystal ball.

Variation

- Explore kitchen utensils and toys as tools to blow bubbles:
  ▸ slotted spoons
  ▸ a clean fly swatter
  ▸ Mason jar lid rings

Crystal Needles

Crystals

Epsom salts molecules line up in an orderly pattern and form needle-shaped *crystals* as the water slowly evaporates from the solution. The salt molecules stack together similar to building blocks. The needle shape of the crystal is determined by the shape of the salt molecule. This is why table salt and Epsom salts do not have the same crystal shapes.

Materials

black paper
scissors
lid from a large jar
1 cup (250 ml) water
4 tablespoons (60 ml) Epsom salts

Art Experiment

1. Cut a circle of black paper that will fit inside the jar lid.
2. Place the circle in the lid.
3. Fill the measuring cup with 1 cup (250 ml) water.
4. Add 4 tablespoons (60 ml) of Epsom salts to the water and stir.
5. Pour the salty water in the lid.
6. Let the mixture in the lid stand for one day. Observe the needle-shaped crystals on the black paper.

Crystal Ink

Crystals / Evaporation

When water *evaporates*, the liquid water changes into a gas or water vapor and enters the air. Dry salt *crystals* are left on the paper because the salt does not evaporate. Heating the paper in the warm oven speeds up the evaporation process. Black paper makes the white crystals easier to see.

Materials

Adult supervision required
oven
3 teaspoons (15 ml) salt
¼ cup (60 ml) water
paintbrush
1 sheet black construction paper

Art Experiment

1. Heat the oven to 150°F (75°C).
2. Add 3 teaspoons (15 ml) salt to ¼ cup (60 ml) water. Stir well.
3. Paint a design or message on the black paper with the salt solution. Stir the salt with the brush each time the brush is used to paint.
5. Turn off the oven and place the paper in the oven on top of the wire racks. Heat for 5 minutes or until the design dries.
6. Remove the dry design from the oven. The design or message will appear as white, shiny crystals.

Plastic Milk

9+

Casein

Milk contains a protein called *casein*. Cheese, made from milk, is mostly casein. Casein is also used to make plastic, glue, and paint. Cooking milk with vinegar causes the casein to separate from the other substances in milk and become a moldable substance similar in characteristics to *plastic*.

Materials

Adult supervision required

10 ounces (0.3 L) milk	old muslin sheet
saucepan	jar
stove	rubber band
spoon	cookie cutter, optional
1 tablespoon (15 ml) vinegar	tempera paint

Art Experiment

1. Warm 10 ounces (0.3 L) of milk in a pan over low heat but do not boil.
2. Add 1 tablespoon (15 ml) vinegar and stir until a white rubbery material forms in the milk. This is called casein.
3. Stretch a square of muslin over the opening of the jar and hold in place with a rubber band around the neck of the jar.
4. Squeeze the milk through the muslin into the jar until the rubbery casein is left.
5. Push the casein into a mold such as a cookie cutter or shape it by hand into any shape.
6. Let it set for a few days so the casein dries and hardens.
7. Decorate the plastic milk with paint

Marshmallow Tower

Engineering

Many bridges and towers are made with triangular shapes. A wide base and narrow top make a sturdy structure. Gravity is always pulling things down towards the Earth. When *engineers* build structures, they are discovering how to keep the structures up.

Materials

package of toothpicks
miniature marshmallows, stale

Art Experiment

1. Stick a toothpick into a stale marshmallow.
2. Add another marshmallow to the other end of the toothpick.
3. Now add another toothpick, another marshmallow, and so on.
4. Keep adding and building until a tower can stand alone.

Variations

- Use modeling clay balls and toothpicks instead of marshmallows.
- Use fruit-colored miniature marshmallows.
- Use gumdrops and toothpicks.

Building Beans

Engineering

Building with beans is a good way to experiment and learn about strong *structures*. *Balance* helps make structures strong. *Gravity* is always pulling things down toward the Earth. When engineers build structures, they are discovering how to keep things up.

Materials

large dried beans
bowl of water
strainer
wooden toothpicks

Art Experiment

1. Soak the beans overnight in the bowl of water.
2. Strain the water off the beans.
3. Stick a toothpick in one bean.
4. Continue sticking beans and toothpicks together to make a structure.
5. When finished, let the bean structure dry overnight.

Variation

- Build a structure with other materials to see which is strongest:
  - balls of clay and toothpicks
  - soaked dry peas and toothpicks
  - fresh peas from the pod and toothpicks

Spaghetti Painting

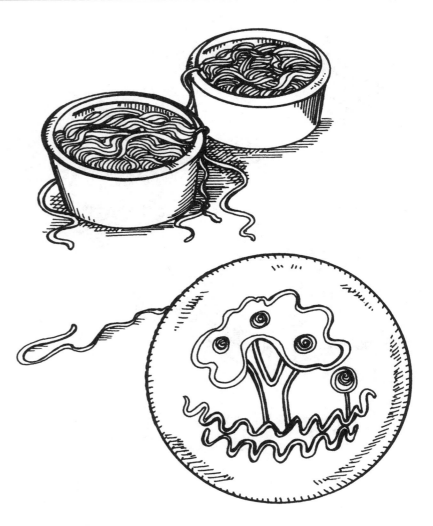

Dissolve / Gluten

Spaghetti is made from flour. Flour on the surface of the spaghetti *dissolves* in the hot water to form its own glue or paste called *gluten*. It can be very sticky. As this natural glue dries, it hardens and bonds the spaghetti to the paper.

Materials

cooked, drained spaghetti
4 glass bowls
food coloring or liquid watercolors
spoons
white paper plates

Art Experiment

1. Place small amounts of cooked, drained spaghetti in four small glass bowls.
2. Add drops of food coloring or watercolors to each bowl, one color for each.
3. Stir until spaghetti is coated with color.
4. Remove a strand of spaghetti from a bowl and arrange on a paper plate in any design.
5. Continue to add more colored spaghetti to the design. Spaghetti will stick without glue.
6. Let the spaghetti picture dry overnight.

Variation

- Cook and color other pastas for "pasta paintings."

3+

Texture

Sandpaper has a rough *texture* that can be examined under a magnifying glass where the individual grains of sand can be seen. Tiny fibers protruding from the yarn snag the grains of sand and stick to the sandpaper.

Materials

sheet of fine sandpaper
pieces of colorful yarn
scissors

Art Experiment

1. Place a sheet of fine sandpaper on the table.
2. Place pieces of colorful yarn on the sandpaper. (Yarn will stick to the sandpaper much like Velcro sticks to itself.)
3. Move yarn pieces to different positions until the design or picture is complete.
4. Take apart and begin again if desired.

Variations

- Sandpaper can be made by covering a sheet of heavy paper with glue and then covering the glue with sand. When completely dry, shake off excess sand.
- Experiment with other items that might stick to the sandpaper, such as lace scraps or embroidery floss.

Invisible Paint

Acid / Base

Many common foods like vinegar and lemon have a sour taste because they contain substances called *acids*. Other foods like milk and baking soda have what are called *bases*. These foods and many other substances have different chemical makeups that make them either *acidic* or a *basic*. Grape juice is an *acid/base indicator*. This means that it will reveal the acid/base level of a substance by changing color. When grape juice touches the baking soda painting, the painting changes from clear to blue-green, indicating that baking soda is a base.

Materials

cups
4 tablespoons (60 ml) baking soda
4 tablespoons (60 ml) water
cotton swab
sheet of white paper
purple grape juice
paintbrush

Art Experiment

1. To make the "paint," dissolve 4 tablespoons (60 ml) of baking soda in 4 tablespoons (60 ml) of water in a cup.
2. Dip the cotton swab in the paint mixture and make a picture on the white paper.
3. Let the watery picture dry completely.
4. Next, brush grape juice over the paper to reveal the painting. The picture mysteriously appears in blue-green colors.

Magic Cabbage

Acid / Base

Many common foods like vinegar and lemon have a sour taste because they contain substances called *acids*. Other foods like milk and baking soda have what are called *bases*. Cabbage juice is an *acid/base indicator*, which means that it will show the acid/base level of a substance by changing color. When vinegar touches the cabbage juice painting, the purple painting changes to pink, indicating that vinegar is an acid.

Materials

Adult supervision required

fresh purple cabbage	water	white paper
knife	strainer	vinegar
pot	bowl	
stove	paintbrush	

Art Experiment

1. Cut the cabbage into small pieces with a knife.
2. Fill a pot half full of water and put the cabbage pieces in it.
3. Have an adult put the pot on the stove and bring to a boil. Boil for about one minute. Then remove it from the heat.
4. Let the pot set for about 20 minutes.
5. Strain the colored cabbage water into a bowl. Set the cabbage aside to eat later.
6. With a paintbrush, use the colored cabbage juice to make a picture on the paper.
7. Let the cabbage juice painting dry completely.
8. Next, brush a little vinegar on the painting to reveal the magic picture. The juice should turn from purple to pink.

Sculptured Pretzels

⚠️ ✋ 🥧 🥣 **4+**

Gases

Yeast in the pretzel dough makes it puff up, or rise. A chemical reaction between the yeast, the flour, and the sugar causes the production of carbon dioxide *gas* that causes the dough to rise. The same kind of gas can be made by mixing baking soda and vinegar, which causes foaming. (See page 94, The Volcano.)

Materials

Adult supervision required

1½ cups (375 ml) warm water	spoon
1 package yeast	greased cookie sheet
1 teaspoon (5 ml) salt	pastry brush
1 tablespoon (15 ml) sugar	1 egg, beaten
4 cups (1 L) flour	salt (optional)
large bowl	oven

Art Experiment

1. Mix up the dough using the following steps:
   - Measure 1½ cups (375 ml) warm water into the large bowl.
   - Sprinkle yeast into water and stir until soft.
   - Add 1 teaspoon (5 ml) salt, 1 tablespoon (15 ml) sugar, and 4 cups (1 L) flour.
   - Mix and knead the dough with hands. Dough should be smooth and elastic, not sticky.
2. To create the sculpture, roll and twist dough into any shapes such as letters, animals, and unique shapes.
3. Place the dough sculptures on a greased cookie sheet.
4. Let rise until double in size.
5. Brush each sculpture with beaten egg.
6. Sprinkle with salt (optional).
7. Bake for 12 to 15 minutes at 350°F (180°C) until sculptures are firm and golden brown. Cool slightly. Eat and enjoy!

CHAPTER 5
Nature and Earth

Bark Rubbings

Bark

The *bark* of a *tree* grows as the tree grows, much like your skin grows with you. Each kind of tree has a bark that helps it live in its enviroment. Some trees have smooth bark, so insects have a hard time holding on and eating the tree. Some trees have thick, rough bark with deep grooves that gives it protection from fires. A Bark Rubbing is a way to see the different patterns of bark that covers and protects trees.

Materials

outdoor space with variety of trees	bucket of water
finger paint	towel
paper	scrub brush

Art Experiment

1. Finger paint on a small area of tree bark.
2. Clean hands.
3. Press and smooth the paper over the painted bark.
4. Slowly peel the paper off the bark and look at the tree bark print. Dry.
5. Meanwhile, wash and scrub the tree bark with clear water and a scrub brush until no trace of paint remains.

Variations

- Make paint rubbings of rocks, leaves, sidewalks, bricks, and other outdoor objects.
- Combine two or three rubbings on one sheet of paper, overlapping textures and paint colors.
- Press imprints of outdoor objects into plasticine or playdough.

Shoe Polish Leaves

5+

Leaves

Leaves come in many beautiful shapes and have interesting patterns on their surfaces. The shape of a leaf helps control the temperature of the plant. The pattern on the leaf's surface is made by veins that carry water and food throughout the plant.

Materials

shoe polish
fresh leaves
old cloth
white paper
brayer or rolling pin

Art Experiment

1. Rub shoe polish on the back of a fresh leaf with an old cloth.
2. Place the leaf polish side down on white paper.
3. Cover the leaf with another piece of white paper.
4. Roll the brayer or rolling pin firmly over the paper-covered leaf.
5. Remove the paper slowly and peel the leaf off by the stem. A leaf print will remain showing veins, stem, and leaf imprint.

Variations

- Use a variety of shoe polish colors and types of leaves.
- Experiment with papers such as tracing paper, waxed paper, textured paper, and colored paper.
- Use ink from an ink pad instead of shoe polish.
- Use paint instead of shoe polish.

Nature Spray

Plants

Plants come in many shapes with many kinds of leaves. The shape in this experiment blocks paint from reaching the paper. When the plant is removed, there will be a *negative* space of the plant remaining. The shape of the plant remains the same, something like a *shadow* or *silhouette* of the natural plant.

Materials

nature collection	paper
pine branches	pencil
leaves	tempera paint in a cup
flowers	toothbrush
screen sieve	table covered with newspaper

Art Experiment

1. Collect a variety of small natural materials such as pine branches, leaves, and flowers.
2. Trace the outside edge of the screen sieve on the paper to make a circle.
3. Make an arrangement of the natural materials inside the sieve's circle on the paper.
4. Gently place the sieve over the arrangement.
5. Dip the toothbrush in the paint and scrape back and forth on the screen of the sieve to make a spray of paint.
6. Continue scraping the toothbrush across the sieve until the paint heavily covers the natural items.
7. Very carefully remove the sieve.
8. Let the nature collection remain in position until the paint is dry, then remove them. Stencils of the branches, leaves, and flowers will be left.

Variations

- Spray paint over:
  - designs cut from paper
  - pieces of masking tape stuck to paper and peeled off when paint is dry
  - small toys and junk items such as Legos, nuts, bolts, and magnetic letters

Plant Imprints

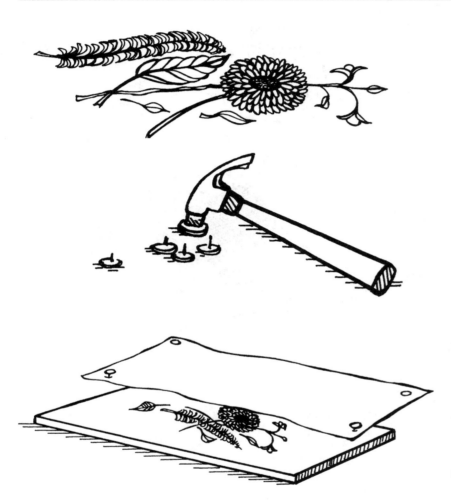

Pigments

The colors seen in fresh leaves and flowers come from chemicals called *pigments*. Crushing the plants with a hammer releases pigments that stain the white fabric. People throughout history have crushed plants and used natural pigments as paint and dye.

Materials

fresh leaves
fresh flowers
white fabric
wooden board
thumbtacks
hammer

Art Experiment

1. Create an arrangement of the leaves and flowers on the wooden board.
2. Tack a piece of white fabric over the arrangement.
3. Next, hammer all over the fabric area crushing the leaves and flowers beneath the fabric.
4. Remove the thumbtacks from the fabric and look at the imprint designs left on the fabric.

Variations

- Cover the plants with a sheet of heavy paper and follow the above hammering process.
- Cover the plants with a sheet of heavy paper and make a plant rubbing with the side of a peeled crayon or stick of charcoal.

Symmetry Prints

⚠️ ✋ 🥧 🖌️ 5+

Symmetry

The apple cut top to bottom shows *bilateral symmetry*. This means that if a line were drawn through the middle of the apple half, the designs and shape of the two sides would match. The apple cut through the middle shows *radial symmetry*. This means that all the designs radiating from the center part of the apple are the same pattern.

Materials

Adult supervision required
2 apples
knife
cutting board
tempera paint in a dish or Styrofoam tray
paper

Art Experiment

1. An adult should cut one apple in half, top to bottom. Then cut another apple in half across the middle.
2. Choose one half from each apple to use for printing with paint, and the other halves to eat.
3. Press the first apple half into paint and then press on paper. Look at the symmetry, which means that the two sides match and are exactly the same in design.
4. Next, press the other apple half into paint and then on to the paper for a different symmetry design.
5. Continue making apple prints in any design desired.

Variations

- Using the apple half cut top to bottom, cut that half in half again, which is a quarter of an apple. The two apple quarters are symmetrical too. Use for prints.
- Try cutting oranges, green peppers, peaches, or pears. Use some symmetrical parts for printing, and some parts for eating.

3+ 🔨 ◔ 🌳 Sticky Pictures

Air

Petroleum jelly is a thick, greasy substance. Small, lightweight materials will stick to a plate covered with petroleum jelly. Studying the airborne materials that land in the sticky jelly is a good way to learn about the *air* we breathe. Some things carried by the air are seeds, spores, pollen, and dust.

Materials

paper plates	petroleum jelly
hole punch	sink, soap, towel
string or yarn	outdoor area

Art Experiment:

1. Punch a hole at the top of the plate and tie a long loop of string or yarn through the hole.
2. Smear petroleum jelly on a paper plate with fingers.
3. Wash and dry hands thoroughly.
4. Hang the plate in an outdoor area, such as from a tree or large bush, clotheline, etc. Leave plate for 2 to 3 days, weather permitting.
5. Bring plate indoors and examine what materials from the air were caught on the jelly on the plate. Observe the patterns.

Variations:

• Hold dandelion seeds and fine grass clippings above the paper plate in your hands and gently blow the seeds into the air so that they land on the paper plate.
• Smear glue on a paper plate and hang it outside to catch airborne bits of things to see what surprises are in the air.

Stencil Leaves

6+

Leaves

Leaves come in many beautiful shapes and have interesting *patterns* on their surfaces. The shape of a leaf helps control the temperature of the plant. The pattern on the leaf's surface is made by veins that carry water and food throughout the plant. Creating Stencil Leaves shows the relationship between beauty and function in nature.

Materials

fresh leaves
glue dots or tape
paper
tempera paint in cups
paintbrushes

Art Experiment

1. Stick leaves to the paper using glue dots or tape.
2. Use the tempera paint and paintbrushes to paint over the leaves and paper. (Paint gently over the edges of the leaves so leaves do not peel off.)
3. Let the painting dry completely (overnight is good).
4. Peel the leaves off of the paper carefully and a natural stencil design will be left on the paper.

Variations

- Trace leaf shapes on old file folders and cut out. Use both shapes for stencils—the leaf and the hole from the cutout leaf.
- Do this art experiment with other shapes or flat objects instead of leaves.
- Spatter paint from a paint brush across the leaves. Cover work area with newspaper and the artist with an apron before beginning. Works well to place paper inside a box with sides to catch spatters.

Tree Arts

8+

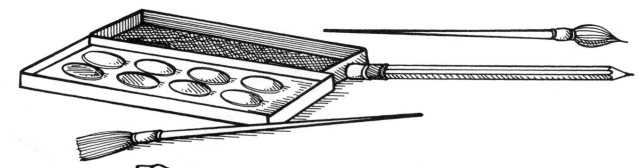

Observation

Scientists and artists both must develop the skill of *observation* or looking closely at things and noting their details. Art and science combine in Tree Arts as the details and characteristics of trees are studied and art is created.

Materials

outdoor area with trees	paintbrushes	pencils
paints	crayons	paper

Art Experiment

The following five ideas are ways to look at trees more closely while creating beautiful art.

1. With the paints and brushes, paint a picture of a tree using just 12 brush strokes.
2. With black paint, paint a silhouette of a tree.
3. Color an entire piece of paper with black crayon. Color hard and bright. Next, scratch a picture of trees in the crayon with a straightened-out paper clip. This is called an etching.
4. Draw or paint leaves while looking at them closely.
5. Use paper and crayon to make rubbings of different tree barks.

Variations

- Save all five art experiments in a booklet stapled together.
- Think of other ways to paint, draw, sculpt, sew, or design tree art.
- An evergreen branch makes a challenging paintbrush.

Indoor Bird Tracks

Animal Tracks / Fossils

Much can be learned from observing *animal tracks*. Sometimes the tracks can tell a story. Scientists who study animal tracks can tell what kind of animal made the tracks, how big it was, and what it was doing when the tracks were made. Sometimes *fossil* animal tracks can be found in very old rock that was once mud. Scientists have learned a great deal about extinct animals like the dinosaurs from these fossil tracks.

Materials

pencil with eraser
ballpoint pen
note cards or paper

Art Experiment

1. Use the ballpoint pen to draw a small bird track on the eraser of an ordinary pencil.
2. Press the eraser down on the note card or paper.
3. Make easy track patterns.
4. When the tracks become hard to see, draw more ink on the eraser with the pen and make more tracks.

Variations

- Design other tiny animal tracks such as mice, gerbils, ants, imaginary creatures, or tiny human feet.
- Make real tracks on large butcher paper by walking in paint and then walking on the paper. Use pretty colors and different kinds of shoes, boots, bare feet, and even skates. Have a tub of water handy for cleanup.
- Find animal tracks in the snow, mud, or sand.

Grass Patterns

Chlorophyll

The green color in plants comes from a substance called *chlorophyll* that helps the plant use sunshine to make energy, much like animals use food to make energy. When the sunlight is blocked, the chlorophyll is reduced and the green color of the grass fades. The grass turns yellow because it cannot survive without light and starts to die. But when sunlight again reaches the grass, the green will return, especially if the grass is also watered.

Materials

cardboard
scissors
patch of grass
rocks or bricks

Art Experiment

1. Cut cardboard shapes from leftover cardboard boxes.
2. Arrange the cardboard shapes on a patch of green grass.
4. Place a rock or brick on each shape to hold it in place.
5. Leave the shapes in place for several days.
6. Then lift the shapes and examine the grass underneath. Notice that the grass looks yellow.
7. The grass will recover slowly and completely as the sun and rain reach the yellow grass. Water the yellowed areas with a hose or sprinkler to speed recovery.

Variations

- Cut letters out of cardboard and spell out words, names, or messages.
- Design a celebration or holiday theme pattern in the grass.

Sand Drawings

Weathering

Sand is made of a variety of crushed and ground materials such as rocks, shells, bones, and plants. The rubbing and bumping together of rocks as wind and water grind them is called *weathering*. Weathered rock will some-day become soil, sand, or be reformed into new rocks.

Materials

dark paper (blue, purple, black, green)
white glue
two rocks (sandstone works very well)

Art Experiment

1. Draw any design on the paper with white glue.
2. Hold two rocks, one in each hand, and rub them together over the paper and glue design. Sand is formed by the rubbing action and will stick in the glue to make a sand drawing.
3. Let sand drawing dry overnight.

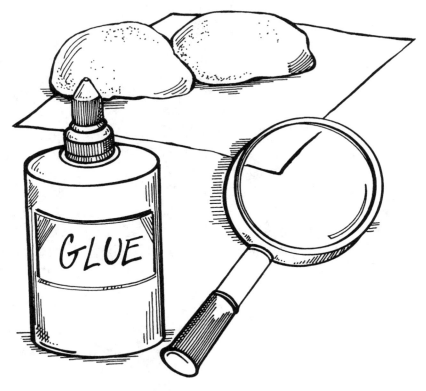

Variations

- Grind sand from the rocks into a box until a ¼ cup (60 ml) or so has been ground. Use a magnifying glass to look at the shapes of the grains of sand. Use this sand to sprinkle on glue to make a sand drawing.
- Pound rocks into powder on a sidewalk or larger rock with a hammer. Wear eye protection. Use the powdered sand to make Sand Drawings.
- Sprinkle sand over a glue drawing. Let dry and shake off extra sand.

Sand Garden

Sand / Rocks

One way sand is made is by crushing or grinding rock into tiny grains that are many different sizes. Some sand grains are so small that they are powdery in *texture*, which can be examined under a magnifying glass. When mixed with water, some of the finest grains of sand make a mud that helps the sand hold together. Sometimes there is a chemical in sand that acts like a glue when mixed with water to help hold the sand grains together. In nature, when sand and water press down very hard for a long time, new rock will be made. One type of rock formed this way is called *sandstone*.

Materials

sandbox

water

plastic cups, containers, boxes

items from nature

rocks

burrs

twigs

Art Experiment:

1. Moisten the sand in the sandbox with water. Stir with hands until sand holds a shape.
2. Pack sand into a container. Then turn it over in the sandbox so the shape comes out in one piece.
3. Add more shapes of sand from packed containers to the sandbox.
4. Decorate the shapes with twigs, rocks, pebbles, burrs, or other items from nature.
5. When complete, save the project or return sandbox to original condition.

Variations

- Create a desert scene using burrs for tumbleweeds and twigs for cactus.
- Create a variety of environments using materials and collections of toys, nature items, etc., such as: mountain, seaside, or park.

Dried Seaweed Print

Plants

Seaweed is a type of plant that grows and lives in the water. By floating seaweed in water and lifting it out on paper, seaweed will keep its natural shape and design.

Materials

shallow pan filled with water	old newspaper
heavy paper	waxed paper or plastic film
fresh seaweed	permanent marking pen, optional

Art Experiment:

1. Sink the heavy paper to the bottom of the shallow pan filled with water.
2. Float a piece of seaweed on top of the paper.
3. Carefully lift out the paper while allowing the water to run off, but keeping the seaweed on the paper.
4. Place the wet paper and seaweed on several thicknesses of newspaper to dry.
5. Cover the paper and seaweed with waxed paper or thin plastic film.
6. Use the permanent pen to write a statement about the seaweed or add additional designs on the plastic film or waxed paper, if desired.
7. Repeat this procedure with other seaweeds, placing each piece of paper and seaweed on top of the first in a stack.
8. When all the seaweeds are stacked, cover with a thick layer of newspaper to absorb excess water.
9. Finally, put the whole stack of papers and seaweeds in a flat place with some weight on top (under a rug is very good).
10. Change the newspapers daily until the seaweed is dry.
11. Peel the waxed paper or plastic film off of the paper and a pressed and dried seaweed display will remain pressed to the waxed paper or plastic film.
12. Display the seaweed print in a window or keep a collection of prints in a notebook.

Dried Arrangement

Rocks

Plaster of Paris is a white powder made from a crushed rock called *gypsum*. Adding water to the powdered crushed gypsum makes a thick paste that can be shaped or poured. When it dries, the plaster of Paris becomes a hard, solid material much like the original gypsum rock. Plaster of Paris is a quick-drying art medium for permanent, rock-like uses.

Materials

Adult supervision required

plant materials	plaster of Paris
dried grasses	water
weeds	paper cups or aluminum pie plates
seed heads	

Art Experiment

1. Collect plant materials in the fall when they are naturally dried in fields and forests.
2. In a paper cup or aluminum pie plate, an adult should mix the plaster of Paris with water as described on the bag (or until like whipped cream).
3. Quickly stick the collected dried weeds, grasses, and seed heads into the plaster like a vase full of flowers. Work quickly, as the plaster of Paris will harden rapidly. (Practice arranging materials in a lump of clay before mixing the plaster if desired.)
4. When complete, allow the arrangement to dry overnight.

Variations

- While flowers and seed stalks are still green, cut them and hang them upside down with string to dry. When dried, use them in the above project instead of grasses and weeds.
- For a more professional flower arrangement, use a flower pot plastic liner that will fit in a basket, small wooden crate, box, or flower pot.

Do not wash plaster of Paris down the drain. It will cause serious clogs.

Nature Windows

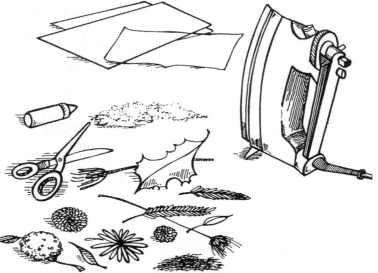

Melting

Waxed paper is just what it sounds like—paper with a coating of wax. The wax on the paper is usually a solid material but *melts* easily into a liquid when heated by the iron, which means the wax molecules flow and move around more freely. If the two sheets of waxed paper are touching when heat is applied from the iron and the molecules are moving about, the wax from one sheet will melt and run together with wax from the second sheet. When the heat is removed, the wax papers cool and the molecules arrange themselves in an orderly pattern. The wax becomes solid again, but the two sheets of waxed paper have fused together into one.

Materials

Adult supervision required

newspapers
table
2 sheets plain paper
2 pieces waxed paper

dried or pressed flowers,
  grasses, leaves
crayon shavings
sand

old iron
scissors

Art Experiment

1. Place a pad of newspaper on the table to protect the table from the heat of the iron.
2. Put one sheet of plain paper on the newspaper.
3. Place one sheet of waxed paper on the plain paper.
4. Arrange dried flowers, grasses, leaves, and crayon shavings in any design on the waxed paper. Finish the design with a tiny sprinkling of sand.
5. Place the second sheet of waxed paper over the design, and the second sheet of plain paper over the waxed paper. Cover all layers with a thin cloth to protect the iron.
6. An adult will press the design with an old iron on a low setting, pressing firmly and slowly. (The two sheets of waxed paper will melt together.)
7. Remove waxed paper design from between papers and trim edges with scissors.
8. Display the design in a window so the light can shine from the outside in during the day, and from the inside out during the dark night.

Garden Sculpture

Germinate

All plants need moisture and sunlight to grow. Grass seeds *germinate* or sprout and start to grow when water soaks into the seed's covering and food is produced in the seed. After the grass seed germinates, it will continue to need water and light to grow and survive.

Materials

small clay saucer (the kind under flower pots)
potting soil
large spoon
grass seed (handful)

spray bottle filled with water
small shells
beeswax
tiny branches

Art Experiment

1. Spoon potting soil into saucer, filling about ¾ full. (Using hands works well too.)
2. Spray soil with the water to moisten.
3. With hands, sprinkle on a good layer of grass seed, but not too thick.
4. Cover the seed with a thin layer of soil.
5. Spray again with water.
6. Place the saucer in a sunny window and watch for signs of growth.
7. Spray the garden once a day.
8. When the garden has sprouted, add other decorations to the sculpture to imitate a miniature garden. Some suggestions are:
   • tiny branch to look like a tree
   • shells to make a pond (fill with water)
   • small animal made from beeswax
   • Stick blossoms of paper on a twig.
   • Add little figurines or toys.
   • Add a "log" made from a small stick.
   • Make a stone path.

Food Paints

Pigment

Foods have natural colorings and dyes called *pigments* that have been used throughout history for coloring clothing or for painting. Pigments are *chemicals* found in food and reflect light the eyes and brain interpret as color. Mixing the foods with water liquifies and thins the foods, making them similar to paints.

Materials

variety of strongly colored spices and foods

- mustard
- cocoa
- curry
- paprika
- blackberries
- beets

muffin tin water

paper paintbrushes

Art Experiment:

1. Put one spice or food in each muffin tin compartment.
2. Add a little water to each compartment and mix well. You may need to crush larger items to release the colors.
3. Dip a paintbrush into the food colors and use them as paint. People once had to make their own art supplies before art stores were available to buy paint sets. Experiment with making paints from spices, vegetables, and berries. Do not eat these homemade paints.
4. Rinse brushes often while painting.

Variations

- Make paintbrushes from broom-straws, grasses, pine boughs, feathers, or sticks.
- Cook some foods to extract their colors for paint. The following foods work well: beet greens, carrot greens, or cranberries.
- Assemble fruits in a basket and try to paint this still life on paper using food paints.

6+ 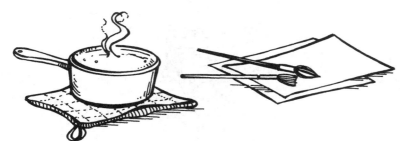 Home Paints

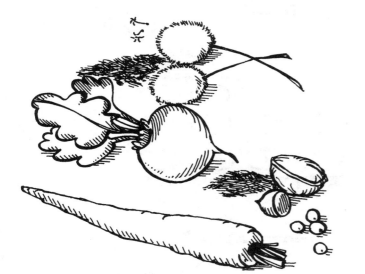

Pigments

The colors seen in the natural world come from chemicals called *pigments*. Pigments are released when the plants are boiled. Since ancient times, plant pigments have been used as dyes for clothes, face paint, and art.

Materials

Adult supervision required

walnut hulls or acorns for brown
onion skins for yellow
beets for red
carrots for orange
grass or spinach for green
cranberries or avocado skins for
  pink

purple grapes for blue
water
stove
sauce pans
paintbrushes
white paper
muffin tin

Art Experiment

1. Boil each of the plants in a separate pan of water until the water turns a deep, pretty color. Cool for a few minutes.
2. Pour the colored waters into separate compartments in the muffin tin.
3. Dip a paintbrush in the colored water and paint on white paper.

Variations

- Paint with colored water on white fabric.
- Place all the plants in one pot for a strong mixed color.
- Collect other natural materials to use as dyes such as tree bark, flowers, weeds, and grasses.

Sand Clay

Bonding

Cornstarch is used in cooking as a thickener. When cornstarch is mixed with sand and water and heated on the stove, the cornstarch works like a cement and thickens the mixture, *bonding* the ingredients as a modeling clay unlike sand alone or cornstarch alone. When an object made from Sand Clay is dried in the oven or left to dry on a shelf, because the cornstarch has bonded with the sand, the object dries to a rock-hard consistency.

Materials

Adult supervision required
1 cup of fine play sand
½ cup (125 ml) cornstarch
½ cup (125 ml) boiling water
double boiler
stove, oven
flat pan or cookie sheet

Art Experiment

1. An adult should mix the fine sand and cornstarch thoroughly in the top of the double boiler on the stove.
2. Next, an adult can pour in the boiling water and mix well.
3. Cook this sand clay mixture in the double boiler briefly until thickened. (If too thick, add a little more boiling water.)
4. Cool the sand clay a bit before modeling. Create any clay designs or objects.
5. Next, place the Sand Clay object on a flat pan in a 275°F (140°C) oven until dry. Or, dry the Sand Clay object for several days on a shelf or table.

Glossary

acid: A material that tastes sour, reacts with bases, and turns purple cabbage juice red. *Invisible Paint 105, Magic Cabbage 106*

adhesion/cohesion: Molecules are attracted to the molecules of other materials by a force called adhesion. Molecules are held together by a stronger force called cohesion. *Candle Coloring 89, White Resist 90*

air: A colorless, odorless, tasteless, gaseous mixture of elements that supports life on Earth. Contains nitrogen, oxygen, other gases, pollutants, and a variety of tiny particles of materials. *Sticky Pictures 116*

attract: Pull toward, as with magnets. *See magnetism.*

base: A material that tastes bitter, reacts with acids, and turns purple cabbage juice green. *Invisible Paint 105, Magic Cabbage 106*

buoyancy: The upward force that a liquid exerts on an object. The force is equal to the weight of the liquid that is pushed aside when the object enters the liquid. *Floating Sculpture 23*

casein: A white plastic-like substance made from milk. *Plastic Milk 100*

centrifugal force: The force on a spinning object from the center (or axis) out and away from the center. *Twirling Rainbow 66*

chlorophyll: Green pigments found in plants that trap energy from sunlight. *Grass Patterns 120*

chromatography: Separating mixtures through an absorbent material at different rates. *Chromatography 92*

condensation: Tiny drops of water on cold things that form when water vapor in the air cools and turns back into water. *See evaporate.*

constellation: A pattern made by stars in the sky. One common constellation is the Big Dipper. *Star Window 57*

crystals: Ice, salt, and many kinds of minerals are all crystals with definite internal structures and external shapes arranged in patterns. *Frost Plate 9, Crystal Sparkle Dough 26, Crystal Design 95, Crystal Paint 96, Crystal Bubbles 97, Crystal Needles 98, Crystal Ink 99*

density: The measurement of the weight of a specific volume; a scientific way to compare the compact character of a material. *Oil & Water Painting 7, Oil Painting 8, Bottle Optics 19, Water Tube 20, Floating Sculpture 23, Clay Floats 24*

diffusion: Spontaneous movement of molecules from one place to another with a uniform mixture resulting. Food coloring diffuses in water. *Wet Paint Design 3, Wet and Dry Painting 4, Color Bottles 17*

dissolve: The complete mixing of a solid in a liquid which then forms a new substance. When sugar dissolves in water, the new substance is sugar water. *Wet and Dry Painting 4, Oil Painting 8, Spaghetti Painting 103*

emulsion: A suspension of small globules of one liquid in a second liquid with which the first will not mix, such as milk fats in milk. *Color Waves 25, Erupting Colors 93*

energy: Power, as shown in action, exertion, performance, or movement. *Shake Picture 63*

engineering: Design, construction, and operation of structures, equipment, and systems. *Marshmallow Tower 101, Building Beans 102*

evaporate: The change from a liquid to a gas by increasing the heat content of the liquid. *Water Painting 6, Paper Molds 22, Crystal Ink 99*

filter: To separate solids or suspended particles from a liquid by passing it through a layer of sand, fiber, or charcoal. Light can also be filtered through colored paper or thin fabric. *Color Viewing Box 55*

freezing point: The temperature at which a liquid solidifies. Water freezes at 32°F (0°C). *Frost Plate 9, Frozen Paper 10,*

Cube Painting 11, Colored Ice Cubes 12, Ice Structures 15, Crystal Paint 96, Crystal Bubbles 97

friction: The resistance met by the rubbing together of one material on the surface of another material. *Paint Racing 64, Polished Crayon 73*

gases: Matter that has low density, expands and contracts readily, and distributes uniformly through any container. *The Volcano 94, Sculptured Pretzels 107*

germinate: To sprout or start to sprout and grow from a seed. Water and sunlight are necessary for germination. *Garden Sculpture 126*

gluten: A glue-like substance found in flour. *Spaghetti Painting 103*

gnomon: The part of a sundial that casts a shadow and helps measure time. *Shadow Time 44*

gravity: The strength of attraction between two objects because of their mass and distance. The Earth's gravity pulls everything toward its center. *Paint Racing 64, Marble Sculpture 69, Paint Pendulum 71, Salt Pendulum 72, Moon Scape 78*

image: The light seen when it bounces off a surface. In a mirror, the reflection bounces off as an image. *See reflection.*

immiscible: Two liquids cannot mix. Oil is immiscible in water. *Immiscibles 91*

inertia: The tendency of something to stay still or keep moving. Gravity and friction affect inertia. *Marble Sculpture 69*

insoluble: Cannot be dissolved or mixed. Oil and water will not mix even when shaken or stirred. *Invisible Designs 5, Oil & Water Painting 7, Oil Painting 8, Color Waves 25*

light: A form of energy; part of the electromagnetic spectrum. *Tissue Color Mix 41, White Color Wheel 42*

liquid: A state of matter where molecules move freely.

magnet: An object that can attract or repel certain materials. *Magnet Painting 81, Funny Faces 82, Metallic Design 83, Magnetic Stage Play 84, Magnetic Designs 85*

magnetic field: The area around a magnet in which the force of the magnet affects the movement of other magnetic objects. *Magnet Painting 81, Funny Faces 82, Metallic Design 83, Magnetic Stage Play 84, Magnetic Designs 85*

magnetism: Invisible force that attracts or repels magnetic materials and has electromagnetic effects.

melting point: The point at which a solid material will begin to turn to a liquid. The melting point of ice is 32°F (0°C). *Cube Painting 11, Colored Ice Cubes 12, Ice Structures 15, Ice & Salt Sculpture 16, Polished Crayon 73, Crayon Creatures 74, Hot Sand Paper 75, Baked Drawings 76, Nature Windows 125*

molecule: The tiny particle produced by the linking of two or more atoms. Everything is made up of tiny particles called molecules.

opaque: Not allowing rays of light to pass through; cannot be seen through. *Silhouettes 51, Silhouette Show 52, Flashlight Patterns 53, Window Scene 58*

optical illusion: The brain "sees" an image in a way that tricks the eye into seeing the object a different way. One common optical illusion is when lines are drawn very close together and they appear to the brain to be moving when they are really holding still. *Spinning Designs 35, Hidden Coloring 36, Secret Pictures 37, Stretch Picture 38, Dot Matrix Picture 37, Face Illusion 40, Streak Spin 65, Moving Pets 67, Spoke Weaving 68*

pendulum: A weighted rod or string fixed at one end that swings freely. *Paint Pendulum 71, Salt Pendulum 72*

photography: The process of creating optical images on photosensitive surfaces, such as on film. *Real Camera 56*

pigments: Any substance or matter used as coloring. Often found naturally in foods and plants used as dyes, inks, and paints. *Tissue Color Mix 41, Plant Imprints 114, Food Paints 127, Home Paints 128*

plants: Any organism, not animal, with cellulose cell walls, that grows, lacks locomotion, and lacks organs or nervous tissue. Usually has roots, blossoms, and leaves and is often green. *Bark Rubbing 111, Shoe Polish Leaves 112, Nature Spray 113, Plant Imprints 114, Stencil Leaves 117, Tree Arts 118, Grass Patterns 120, Dried Seaweed Print 123, Dried Arrangement 124, Garden Sculpture 126, Food Paints 127, Home Paints 128*

pointillism: An art technique of applying paint in small dots or points to the paper in order to create an effect of optical mixing. *Dot Matrix Picture 37*

pressure: Force applied over a surface or the application of continuous force. *Bottle Fountain 18, Crystal Sparkle Dough 26, Straw Painting 27, The Volcano 94*

reflection: The light or image seen when light bounces off a surface. *See It Cards 43, Infinity Reflection 45, Mirror Painting 46, Flashlight Reflections 54, Bubble Sculpture 59*

repel: To push away, as with magnets. *See magnetism.*

rocks: Any relatively hard, naturally formed mass of minerals or petrified material. Sand is mostly crushed or ground up rock. *Sand Drawings 121, Sand Garden 122, Sand Clay 129*

solid: A substance that is compact; not liquid.

soluble: Can be dissolved, such as salt in water. *Wet and Dry Painting 4, Erupting Colors 93*

solution: Liquid containing a dissolved substance. *See dissolve.*

spectrum: The colors found in white light—red, orange, yellow, green, blue, indigo, and violet. *White Color Wheel 42*

static electricity: A buildup of negative charges called electrons. Static means it stays in one place, unlike current electricity, which can flow through things. *Balloon Decoration 79, Dancing Rabbits 80*

sundial: A tool for telling the time on a sunny day by the shadows cast each hour. *Shadow Time 44*

surface tension: The stretchy skin of a liquid which is caused by the attraction of molecules on its surface. *Chalk Float Design 14, Color Waves 25*

symmetry: Balance, matching arrangement of pattern, or equal and exact matching. *Flowing Patterns 21, Symmetry Prints 115*

texture: The appearance and feel of something. Sandpaper has a rough texture. A mirror has a smooth texture. *Sandpaper Designs 104*

time: A way to measure an hour, day, month, or year based on the rotation and revolution of the Earth. *Shadow Time 44*

translucent: Light can shine through but cannot be seen through. *Window Scene 58, Nature Windows 125*

transparent: Light can shine through and can be seen through. *Flashlight Patterns 53, Nature Windows 125*

water vapor: Tiny droplets of water in the air too small to see and formed by evaporation. *See evaporate.*

weathering: The grinding action that makes sand. *Sand Drawings 121*

white light: A band of seven different colors—red, orange, yellow, green, blue, indigo, and violet. Each color has a different wavelength. All the colors mixed together make white light. *White Color Wheel 42*

wind: Movement of air. *Streamer Rings 28, Wind Catcher 29, Windy Wrap 30, Wind Chime 31*

Index